OUTLAW TALES
of Nebraska

True Stories of the Cornhusker State's
Most Infamous Crooks, Culprits, and Cutthroats

T. D. Griffith

TWODOT

GUILFORD, CONNECTICUT
HELENA, MONTANA
AN IMPRINT OF GLOBE PEQUOT PRESS

A · TWODOT® · BOOK

Copyright © 2010 Morris Book Publishing, LLC

Project editor: David Legere
Map: M.A. Dubé © Morris Book Publishing, LLC

Library of Congress Cataloging-in-Publication Data
Griffith, T. D. (Tom D.), 1958-
  Outlaw tales of Nebraska : true stories of the Cornhusker State's most infamous crooks, culprits, and cutthroats / T.D. Griffith.
    p. cm.
  Includes bibliographical references and index.
  ISBN 978-0-7627-5878-4
  1. Outlaws—Nebraska—Biography—Anecdotes. 2. Criminals—Nebraska—Biography—Anecdotes. 3. Frontier and pioneer life—Nebraska—Anecdotes. 4. Nebraska—History—Anecdotes. 5. Nebraska—Biography—Anecdotes. I. Title.
  F666.6.G75 2010
  364.3–dc22

                                        2010022015

Printed in the United States of America

10 9 8 7 6 5 4 3 2 1

For my favorite mother-in-law Bonnie
who probably knew all these guys.

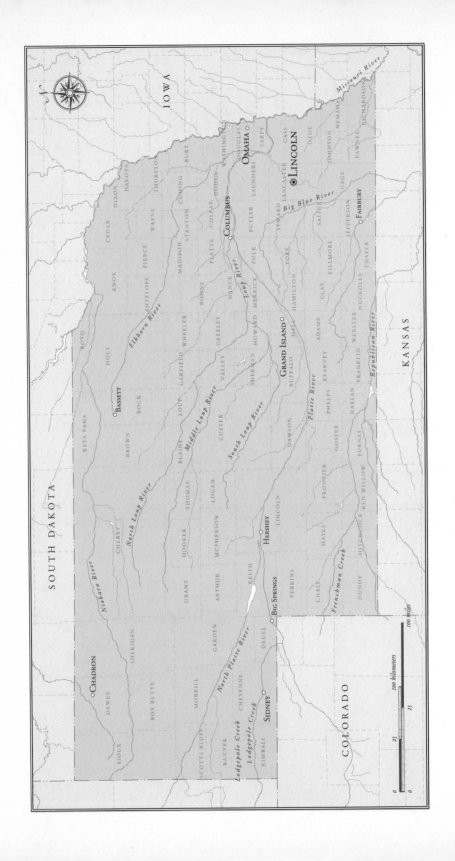

Contents

Acknowledgments

If history truly is "a fable agreed upon," as Napoleon Bonaparte contended, then this work is the result of a variety of individuals, organizations, and institutions which have endeavored to capture the real-life stories of Nebraska's crooks, cutthroats, swindlers, and rogues.

Outlaw Tales of Nebraska could not have been written without the able assistance and valuable direction of numerous people, including my friends doctors Bob and Char Wilson; Navy hero and Nebraska state treasurer Shane Osborn; former Nebraska secretary of state and current Nebraska Press Association executive director Allen J. Beermann; and Evelyn Dalao and Ann Fagerberg at the Bennett Martin Public Library in Lincoln, Nebraska.

So many staff members at Nebraska's museums provided insight and knowledge of the characters and criminals who are inexorably linked to this state's past, including Jessica Waite and Duane Witt, two history lovers at the remarkable Stuhr Museum of the Prairie Pioneer in Grand Island; Michelle Gullett at the *Omaha World-Herald*; Erin McDanal and Elena Cline of the Colorado State Archives; Tiffany Sherwood and Vern Pfaff at First National Bank in Fairbury; and the dedicated staff of the Nebraska State Historical Society, particularly Mary-Jo Miller, Curt Peacock, Andrea Faling, and Cindy Drake.

Special thanks to my longtime friends, Mary Kopco, director of the exceptional Adams Museum and House in Deadwood, South Dakota; and Jeanette Moodie, director of Deadwood

Public Library, for their warm smiles and gentle guidance. Thanks, too, to Meredith Rufino, my editor at TwoDot/Globe Pequot Press, whose contributions are found in the copyright date and on every page.

And, finally, appreciation is extended to my wife and fellow author, Nyla, who knows that there's a little outlaw in each of us.

Introduction

With its wide-open spaces, free-running rivers, and grasslands that stretch to the sky, Nebraska has been attracting the notable and the unknown for centuries.

The Pawnee and Omaha first hunted here, stalking buffalo that once blanketed the Great Plains. Spaniard Francisco Vázquez de Coronado and his band of explorers likely passed through what is now the state of Nebraska as early as 1541. When the Louisiana Purchase ceded the land from France to the United States in 1803, the transaction brought Lewis and Clark's Corps of Discovery through the next year and, soon, fur traders, steamboats, and sodbusters stormed the Nebraska Territory.

While the first European explorers labeled the region the "Great American Desert," Nebraska would become one of the leading agricultural areas in the world. Eventually four historical trails—the Lewis and Clark, Oregon, Mormon, and Pony Express—would crisscross what would initially be known as "The Tree Planter State." Indeed, these trails all headed elsewhere, to points further west, but thousands of homesteaders, miners, merchants, and madams found Nebraska to their liking and decided to stay.

The Kansas-Nebraska Act of 1854 established both territories. After Congress carved out the Dakota and Colorado territories in 1863, Nebraska became the sixteenth state in the United States on March 1, 1867. Since then, the Cornhusker State has given the world an assortment of characters, including Fred Astaire, Marlon Brando, Johnny Carson, Gerald Ford, and Malcolm X, and modern marvels ranging from Kool-Aid and the Reuben sandwich to 911 emergency response and Carhenge. As testament to the enduring patriotism of Nebraskans, 40 percent of the ammunition used by the U.S. in World War II was manufactured at the Naval Ammunition Depot in the small town of Hastings.

But, before the arrival of the railroads, and the construction of too many churches, outlaws reached Nebraska to pursue what they generally do—rob, wreck, rustle, and eradicate anyone who stood in their way. By and large, the law came late to this Midwestern frontier, save for a few marshals, bounty hunters, and Pinkerton agents. That meant cattle rustlers, horse thieves, train robbers, bank bandits, and your run-of-the-mill murderers tended to operate with relative impunity until the haul got large enough to notice or the bodies started stacking up like cordwood.

By their very nature, the lawbreakers of Nebraska's past did their best to remain elusive. They generally didn't pose for pictures or sit for extended interviews with the liberal media. Retracing the prints of horse's hooves and the tracks of getaway cars and bullet holes—sometimes decades or even centuries after the fact—is not without its challenges or contradictions. Suffice it to say, in this work we have endeavored to separate the real from the imagined and present the facts, as disheartening, shocking, and cruel as some of the crimes may have been.

Come along on this trail of tears, of crooks, culprits, and cutthroats, of men and a few women so full of bluster and blow that they'd as soon steal your favorite horse or rob your life's savings as tip their hat in greeting. From an Omaha chief who had a deadly means of dealing with challengers, and a succession of raucous rustlers and robbers, to hatchet murderers, sniper maniacs, and America's first serial killer, they've all wandered Nebraska's flatlands.

These, then, are their stories—the *Outlaw Tales of Nebraska.*

Blackbird's Gruesome Game

As leader of one of North America's most powerful tribes in the late eighteenth century, Omaha chief Blackbird encountered many challengers. Like a bull elk in autumn, Blackbird locked antlers with innumerable foes who sought his power and his prestige. But, unlike those who sought to command his people, the most dominant tribe on the Great Plains, the wily chieftain pulled no punches; instead, he employed poison to defeat his rivals. He performed dastardly acts that would create a legend and Nebraska's first outlaw.

As he was known to his people, Wazhinga-sah-ba was fearsome, brave in battle, and possessed strong "medicine" that allowed him to foil his foes. Blackbird was, however, not without his faults. When a favored wife embarrassed him in front of his tribe, he hastily threw a knife at her, killing her where she stood. As chief in a lawless land not yet settled by whites, his only punishment came not from the courts, but from his own lingering conscience.

Assuming control over the Omaha tribe in the late 1770s, Blackbird was among the first Native American leaders to establish trade agreements with the Spanish and French fur traders who roamed what was then the Western frontier, now the state of Nebraska. Under Blackbird's leadership, the Omaha also became the first tribal warriors on the Great Plains to master the fine art of equestrianism, which, for a brief period, allowed his people dominance over the Lakota Sioux and other major Plains Indian tribes.

Although his tribe was not as large as other clans in the region, Chief Blackbird's skill in establishing favorable relations with white traders and explorers further helped the Omaha fend off other warring tribes for the more than three decades that he remained in power.

In 1600, more than 170 years before Blackbird rose to chief, evidence indicates the Omaha had begun as a much larger woodland tribe comprised of both Quapaw and Omaha bands, inhabiting a vast tract between the Ohio and Wabash rivers. The bands eventually migrated westward, and the Omaha split from the Quapaw. When French cartographer Guillaume Delisle stumbled on the "wandering nation" of "the Maha" in 1718, he found them along the northern stretch of the Missouri River. Two decades later, French fur traders located the tribe on the west banks of the river, near present-day Cedar County, Nebraska.

Sometime around 1755, the tribe established the new village of "Ton won tonga" (translated as "Big Village") near the Missouri River in extreme northeastern Nebraska, north of the present-day Omaha Indian Reservation. This would be the home of Chief Blackbird and as many as 4,000 members of his tribe. And, a century later, the largest city in Nebraska would be named Omaha, for the powerful tribe that never was known to take up arms against the United States.

As a young brave, Blackbird reportedly proved his worth in a number of skirmishes against competing tribes. Captured by the Sioux as a boy, he escaped and later fought them and other tribes until all inhabitants of the region feared his name and his reputation. He purportedly took scalps from the Otoe and Kansas tribes, burned a Pawnee village to the ground, and employed strange "medicine" that allowed him to overcome the enemies of the Omaha.

According to the late Nebraska historian, Addison Erwin Sheldon, Blackbird was once in pursuit of a hostile war party when he fired his rifle into the hoofprints of their horses, telling his band the unusual action would cripple their horses and allow them to be overtaken. When Blackbird and his warriors did indeed overtake their enemies and slay them all, the Omaha were convinced of the strength of Blackbird's medicine.

Further enhancing Blackbird's reputation as a fierce rival was an incident involving the Ponca Indians who lived as neighbors of the Omaha near the mouth of the Niobrara River. Although the two tribes were related and spoke similar languages, conflicts occasionally occurred that needed to be addressed. When a band of young Ponca men raided the Omaha encampment, stealing horses and kidnapping a few Omaha women, Blackbird's response was swift and decisive.

Gathering all the fighting men of the Omaha, Blackbird led them against the raiders and quickly began "to eat up the Poncas," according to Sheldon. When the vastly outnumbered Poncas were eventually cornered in a crude fort, a furious Blackbird and his warriors were ready to kill them all.

"The Poncas sent a herald carrying a peace pipe," Sheldon wrote before his death in 1943. "Blackbird shot him down. Another herald was treated in the same way. Then the head chief of the Poncas sent his daughter, a young girl, in her finest Indian suit of white buckskin, with the peace pipe. Blackbird relented, took the pipe from the girl's hand, smoked it and there was peace between the tribes."

The beautiful Ponca maiden eventually would become

the favored wife of the Omaha's fiercest fighter and legendary leader, wielding great influence in Blackbird's lodge and in his dealings with fellow tribesmen. But, it would be short-lived. When his Ponca wife angered Blackbird over some minor transgression, the chief flew into a fit of rage and hastily drew his knife from its scabbard and plunged it into the handsome maiden, instantly killing her. As his anger turned to grief over what he had done, Blackbird buried his head in a buffalo robe, slumped down near his wife's body, and refused to sleep or eat for days. Entreaties from his tribesmen were met with silence, and all around him feared they were witnessing the last days of their leader.

In a final act of desperation, another tribal head carried a small child to Blackbird and laid it on the ground before him, placing the chief's foot upon the child's neck. The tender gesture apparently touched Blackbird's heart, for he threw off the buffalo robe, shed his sorrow, and resumed his duties as chief of the Omaha Nation.

As French and Spanish explorers and fur traders tracked across their territories on the Great Plains of North America in ever-increasing numbers in the late 1700s, the free-roaming herds of buffalo began to dwindle. Blackbird was prescient enough to know that the white man's culture was wending its way across the prairie like a gathering storm. Reluctant to migrate further west as many of his brethren had done, Blackbird instead made a conscious effort to create a trading relationship with the newcomers. In this, he was not beneficent, only insightful.

Living on the banks of the Mighty Missouri and in the deep, surrounding coulees that afforded protection, the Omaha had developed a sophisticated society based on the inseparable union between the earth and the sky. Divided into two *moieties*, or kinship groups, Sky people attended to the tribe's spiritual needs, while the Earth people focused on the physical welfare of the tribe by hunting, fishing, and fighting off other bands.

In winter, Omaha tribesmen lived in villages consisting of timber-framed lodges covered with thick soil. Some lodges measured 60 feet in diameter and were capable of accommodating several families and a few treasured ponies. In summer, the Omaha often adopted the ways of the Sioux, hunting migrating herds of buffalo by day and sleeping in tepees at night.

It was into this well-established society in the latter years of the eighteenth century that French fur traders and Spanish explorers first strode, rode, and steamed with a collection of Western paraphernalia that dazzled the native inhabitants. No Omaha was more astonished by the variety of material goods and wonderful elixirs than was Chief Blackbird.

Shrewd, clever, and never shy about taking advantage of his position, Blackbird customarily greeted traders personally and then invited them to his lodge. Traders were directed to assemble all their goods and spread them out in the spacious lodge of the chief. According to historian Sheldon, Blackbird would then select the very best items for himself—warm blankets, colorful beads, and fine tobacco, as well as whiskey, powder, and bullets—and place them to the side, with no expectation of compensating the trader.

Summoning an underling, the chief would order him to climb atop the lodge and tell the entire tribe to collect their furs and come trade with the friendly white man. Shortly, the lodge would be crowded with anxious Indians bearing piles of buffalo robes, beaver pelts, and otter skins.

"No one was allowed to dispute the prices fixed by the white trader, who was careful to put them high enough to pay five times over for all the goods taken by the chief," Sheldon wrote. "Thus Blackbird and the traders grew rich together, but his people grew poor and began to complain."

Faced with increasing dissent created by his own greed after three decades of dictatorial leadership, Blackbird feared for his exalted position at the top of the tribe. Obviously aging and no longer the fine physical specimen he'd been in his youth, he was likely viewed with suspicion by his people for his close relationship with white settlers. Nonetheless, Blackbird had grown accustomed to the perks of being at the peak of his power, and he had no desire to change the status quo.

Consequently, when a friendly trader suggested a magical solution to get rid of those who would oppose his power or question his directives, Blackbird immediately grasped his proposition and reveled in the conspiracy. In his ongoing quest to maintain power, the chief accepted a large amount of arsenic from the trader, who provided helpful suggestions for how it might best be used. Thus began the legendary Omaha chief's deadly plan to thwart any and all rivals.

About the same time, one of five European expeditions to explore the Upper Missouri River, prior to Lewis and Clark's fabled Corps of Discovery, stumbled on the Omaha tribe in present-day Nebraska. The Spanish expedition's leader, Jean Baptiste Truteau, operating under the charter of the Company of Discoverers and Explorers of the Missouri, commonly known as the Missouri Company, sought to reach the Mandan villages of present-day North Dakota and establish a trading post.

Although Truteau failed to reach the Mandan, only traveling as far as present-day South Dakota, he did return from the Western frontier with journals that would later aid Lewis and Clark in planning their journey to the Pacific, as well as a candid assessment of the notorious Omaha chieftain known as Wazhinga-sah-ba. After meeting Blackbird on December 18, 1794, Truteau wrote:

> This great chief of the Omahas was the most shrewd, the most deceitful and the greatest rascal of all the nations who inhabit the Missouri. He is feared and respected and is in great renown among all strange nations, none of whom dare to contradict him openly or to move against his wishes . . . [H]e is a man who by his wit and cunning has raised himself to the highest place of authority in his nation and who has no parallel among all the savage nations of this continent. He is able to or cause to be done good or evil as it pleases him. It is not his war-like actions that have brought him so much power, for he has been inclined towards peace, but because of the fear that his men and his neighbors have of certain poisons which he uses, they say to kill off those who displease him.

As his reputation expanded beyond his own people and neighboring tribes to include white settlers stretching their tentacles across the land, Blackbird grew more emboldened and decidedly more deadly. Armed with a mysterious power and an innate desire to maintain control over his tribe, Blackbird became a prophet as well as a chief.

When younger, stronger, wiser, or nobler contenders for the position of chief arose, Blackbird would simply counter their logical succession by foretelling of the rival's death within a specified time. Indeed, when the challenger would inexplicably suffer a sudden and agonizing death, tribal members were astounded by Blackbird's abilities to see the future and safeguard the well-being of the tribe. Not surprisingly, in short order, all of Blackbird's rivals disappeared and his people, undoubtedly fearing his deadly gaze, acquiesced to the chief's every whim and desire. There were no critics to be found.

Secure in his leadership and surrounded by loyal tribal members, Blackbird would live a few more years in absolute power atop the most dominant tribe on the Plains. But, in the earliest years of the nineteenth century, an enemy arrived among the Omaha that was destined to decimate the tribe, divert history, and deal Blackbird a challenge from which Nebraska's first outlaw would never recover. And, in a strange twist of fate, it was delivered by the same white man that Blackbird had befriended.

Smallpox, the scourge of the Native peoples who populated the Americas, first arrived in the New World with Europeans and Africans in the sixteenth century. The first major outbreak occurred between 1616 and 1619 on the northeastern Atlantic coast, when smallpox reduced the Algonquin tribes from an estimated 30,000 members to 300.

As the newcomers to America headed west over the ensuing centuries, so too did the spread of the infectious disease. Without any prior exposure or resistance to smallpox, Plains Indian tribes such as the Omaha were faced with an invisible enemy that even Blackbird's strange and powerful "medicine" couldn't counter. The effect would be devastating.

Although Natives would also suffer from other deadly diseases that included cholera, bubonic plague, influenza, measles, typhus, and yellow fever, those diseases combined didn't kill as many American Indians as did the smallpox epidemic. According to widely accepted estimates, the epidemic killed more than a third of the Aztecs; half of the Cherokee, Huron, Catawba, Piegan, and Iroquois; two-thirds of the Blackfeet and Omaha; nine out of ten Mandan; and all of the Taino.

Baffled by a faceless enemy that could mysteriously travel from lodge to lodge and village to village, the unwelcome visitor finally arrived at Chief Blackbird's well-established town of Ton won tonga in 1800. Before it departed, smallpox would take the lives of more than 400 of the defenseless Omaha. According to historian Sheldon, in a matter of months, smallpox had decimated the entire tribe.

> This was smallpox, the white man's disease which the
> Indians had never known. It came among them like a
> curse . . . The fever and the fearful blotches drove them
> wild. Some of them left their villages and rushed out on
> the prairies to die alone. Others set fire to their houses
> and killed their wives and children. Two-thirds of the
> Omaha tribe perished and it never after recovered its old
> strength and power.

Eventually, even the old warhorse was stricken. As friends and eager successors gathered around his deathbed, Chief Blackbird delivered his final command: a desire to be buried seated on his favorite steed at the summit of a hill overlooking the Missouri River.

When he had taken his last breath, the Omaha obeyed their chief's dying order, placed his corpse on the back of his horse, led it up the hill, then buried both under a great mound of earth and rocks. A pole bearing the scalps Blackbird had taken in battle was placed at the top of the mound. Four years later, when Lewis and Clark passed through the Omaha village on their epic journey to the Pacific, the explorers climbed what forever after has been known as Blackbird Hill—a lingering reminder of Nebraska's first, and perhaps, deadliest outlaw.

Sam Bass
Scourge of the Plains

The exploits of Sam Bass have spawned more than legend and lore. Indeed, one of Nebraska's most famous outlaws has been remembered during the century since his violent death with cowboy ballads, frontier celebrations, wax statues, community theater performances, and shoot-outs.

In life, Sam Bass was a man to be feared. Although he wasn't born nor did he die in Nebraska, the Sam Bass story was talked about in smoke-filled saloons and civilized salons of the late 1800s from the Dakota Territory to Mexico. Sam Bass staged his most ambitious and lucrative score in the Cornhusker State—a train robbery that brought in more gold pieces than one could possibly carry, creating a Western legend that lives to this day. Finally, it was Nebraska's quiet, creek-carved coulees and slow-rolling prairies that provided refuge for Bass and his roving band of outlaws, lying low after a stagecoach holdup.

Born to Daniel and Elizabeth Jane (Sheeks) Bass on July 21, 1851, on a quiet farmstead near Mitchell, Indiana, Bass was orphaned before he became a teenager. By some reports, Bass spent five years with an abusive uncle before the lure of the American West caused him to run away in 1869. He reached Rosedale, Mississippi, where he spent the winter working in a sawmill. In his idle time, Bass perfected his poker game and learned to wield a sidearm.

Joining forces with a teamster he had befriended, Bass headed for open cattle country on horseback the next summer, and spent the fall and winter of 1870 working on a ranch outside Denton, Texas. He quickly found that the daily rigors of ranch life amounted to hard, even backbreaking work. Punching cows, fixing fences, and braving the elements simply didn't add up to the romantic existence everyone was reading about in the dime-store novels of the day. Indeed, for Bass, it was thankless toil that seemed to never end.

Not in love with the isolation of the rural ranch, Bass headed into town where he found work with Sheriff W. F. "Dad" Egan, cutting firewood, tending livestock, building fences, and running freight between Denton and the new railroad centers at Dallas and Sherman. To make ends meet, the young Sam Bass also handled horses in the stables of the Lacy House, a local hotel.

Riding horses, milking cows, pushing freight, and traveling a lonesome trail for the local sheriff gave Bass moderate experience and plenty of time to think about his future. Perhaps he thought he could do better. Squirreling away his earnings, the uneducated but thrifty Bass began to develop a master plan for financial independence that didn't include cow udders, wood axes, heavy lifting, or horse manure. He only needed the right champion charger to jump-start his newest career.

By 1874, the twenty-three-year-old Bass had become increasingly interested in horse racing. With his savings, he bought himself a powerful fifteen-hand horse known as the "Denton Mare." Quitting his dead-end job with the local sheriff, the last legitimate work he would ever perform, Bass trained his horse, took on all comers, and raced his way to early success. He won the majority of his races in north Texas, and pursued prize purses as far away as San Antonio. His winnings allowed him idle time to ingest copious quantities of alcohol and entertain sultry upstairs girls in Denton's finest saloons. But, by 1876, the buzz over horse racing had diminished, and Bass was forced to return to reality and the trail.

Teaming up with another cowboy, Joel Collins, the pair gathered a small herd of longhorn cattle from local ranchers and agreed to drive them to market in Dodge City, Kansas. When they arrived in Dodge, trailing their dusty herd, Bass and Collins learned that prices for cows were better further north, so they kept on moving, right into the annals of Nebraska outlaw history.

After Bass and Collins had sold the entire herd at a premium price and paid the hands who had accompanied them on the drive, the pair found they still had the princely sum of $8,000 in their possession. The temptation proved too much, and, rather than return south to Texas to settle up with the ranchers, the two headed north, where they partook in several whiskey-induced weeks of wicked women and tireless gambling in Ogallala, Nebraska, and the booming gold-rush town of Deadwood, Dakota Territory. In short order, the ill-gotten gains that had recently filled their pockets had evaporated like a summer thunderstorm on the parched plains.

Busted and thirsty in the Black Hills in 1877, Bass and Collins tried their hands at prospecting, all the rage in the gold-filled gulch of Deadwood. They soon found that standing knee-deep in an ice-cold mountain creek, bent over, panning for any trace of "color" in the gray gravel of the streambed, was even less captivating than driving bawling cows across the endless prairie.

So the pair turned to freighting, where they were even less successful. In forming their small freighting company, they did, however, notice the value of the cargo they were hauling, and the worldly possessions of the stagecoach passengers who passed them on the rutted frontier trails. Just like the earlier cows-for-cash conspiracy, the well-dressed stagecoach passengers would prove to be just one more step on Sam Bass's criminal trail to torment and an early grave.

Desperate, the partners recruited several other bad men and decided to become desperadoes. Drawn to the "treasure coaches" transporting gold bullion for the Homestake and other Black Hills gold mines, Bass and his boys drew their bead on the mother lode. They knew that all of the refined gold gathered from the ground in this ancient mountain range must be moved somewhere—to trading centers such as Cheyenne, Wyoming, Denver, Colorado, and Valentine, Nebraska. And, because the Black Hills were not yet served by the railroad, the valuable cargo had to be hauled in wagons or stagecoaches.

Joined by the heavily armed Frank Towle, Robert "Little Reddy" McKimie, and another man known as Nixon, Bass and Collins laid plans for their big score.

On the evening of March 25, 1877, the Collins-Bass gang (as it would later come to be known) assembled on horseback amid the gathering darkness of Whitewood Canyon. In the coolness of the late-winter night, they checked their weapons and whispered their dark plans for the Deadwood-bound stage, expected anytime.

A few miles away, twenty-six-year-old Johnny Slaughter was driving the Cheyenne and Black Hills stage pulled by a six-horse hitch toward Deadwood. Beside Slaughter on the boot sat Walter Iler, a traveling salesman for an Omaha distillery. According to Barbara Fifer, author of *Bad Boys of the Black Hills*, the stage driver was extremely popular and had a wide circle of friends in Deadwood and Cheyenne. He also happened to be the son of Cheyenne city marshal John N. Slaughter.

"Slaughter was driving hard to make up for lost time after some delays in Hill City," Fifer wrote. "When the road agents brought the stage to a halt in Whitewood Canyon, McKimie was standing near the lead horses, the first of three pairs pulling the coach. The overheated animals were nervous and started moving about, so McKimie fired his shotgun, putting a circle of buckshot around Slaughter's heart, a few pieces of shot into Iler's arm, and another through the coat sleeve of a second passenger."

With the shotgun blast echoing off the canyon walls in the still of the night, the horses bolted, Slaughter's body fell to the ground from the stagecoach, and the injured Iler fought to control the team. Managing to bring the horses under his charge, Iler drove the stage onto the muddy Main Street of Deadwood about midnight. Learning of the assault on Slaughter from Iler and the passengers, a posse of friends and lawmen quickly formed to pursue the raiders.

In the ensuing days, the Collins-Bass gang would learn that one of the passengers of the coach had been carrying $15,000, and that the community leaders of Deadwood had posted a $500 reward for the capture of any of the criminals. With nothing to show for their efforts, save a wanted poster, they were ready to kill Little Reddy for firing his shotgun. Instead, they merely kicked him out of the gang and told him to leave the Hills forever. McKimie simply hooked up with another gang and committed a host of other heists. He was later arrested and jailed after committing robberies in Ohio and Kentucky.

But the Collins-Bass gang continued their Black Hills crime spree, pulling off a half-dozen more stage robberies in 1877. In none of them did they claim a major score, and they never recouped the small fortune the trail drivers had made and then blown on their illegal cattle sale the previous year. With other gangs frequenting the remote trails of the Deadwood area and mining companies hiring added security to guard their shipments, pickings were slim, and it didn't look like things would improve for the hapless outlaws.

Tired of the puny payoffs from stagecoach holdups, the "Black Hills Bandits" (as they were variously known) turned their collective heads south, toward the trains carrying valuable goods, gold, and well-heeled rail users. After losing McKimie and adding James Berry and Jack Davis, they numbered six.

Just before 11:00 p.m. on September 18, 1877, with a full moon lighting the prairie around the station in Big Springs, Nebraska, 10 miles east of the Colorado border, the crooks crept into the rail yard and forced the stationmaster to signal the oncoming Union Pacific express train to stop. When it did, the outlaws forcibly boarded the train. They discovered only $450 in the "way safe," so they viciously beat the express messenger in an attempt to gain entry into the "through safe." Unfortunately, that stronghold featured a time lock that prevented it from being opened until the train had reached its intended destination.

Stymied by the lock and afraid they'd come up short one more time, the armed thieves began searching the train cars, eventually securing $1,300 and a fine collection of gold jewelry from the passengers. Then they struck it rich. Noticing some wooden boxes, the outlaws broke them open and found they were filled with $20 gold pieces, fresh from the San Francisco Mint. All told, the bonanza would net the gang more than $60,000, their biggest haul and, purportedly, still the largest robbery in the history of the Union Pacific.

Despite the initial haul, the results of the daring and lucrative train robbery would be decidedly mixed. After each collecting $10,000 and change, the Collins-Bass gang split up into three parties. Collins and his partner were cornered and killed by lawmen attempting their arrest a week after the heist. Berry and Nixon took a different path with varied outcomes. Berry was captured and jailed, while Nixon escaped and was later assumed to be living a comfortable life in Canada.

Meanwhile, Sam Bass and Jack Davis reportedly traded in their saddles for a one-horse-buggy ride south, their stash stowed neatly beneath the seat. According to one source, during their slow trip to Texas, Bass and Davis were joined on the trail for four days by detectives and a company of soldiers searching for the train robbers. The bandits were able to convince the lawmen and officers that, coincidentally, they also were searching for the culprits in hopes of collecting a substantial reward.

Back home in Denton, just two years after he had left to pursue horse racing, Bass explained his newfound wealth by saying he had struck it rich in the Black Hills gold rush. Bass was briefly the center of attention in the small town of Denton, and he attracted many friends. Some would later assist him in robbing trains across Texas, because robbing trains and grabbing other people's gold was now in Sam Bass's blood.

On February, 22, 1878, the newly christened Sam Bass Gang hit the Texas Central Train at Allen Station. Four weeks later, they struck the same train again, this time at Hutchins. Three weeks later, Bass and his boys boarded the Texas & Pacific Railroad at Eagle Ford, and then robbed it again six days later at Mesquite. The $1,300 they commandeered in the first holdup was the only haul of any consequence, and word leaked out that they had missed major stashes of money hastily hidden by express messengers on two of the trains. The amateurish and almost comical robberies caused some observers to remark that the gang was either drunk or extremely nervous in the commission of their crimes.

Always one to welcome attention, Sam Bass got it now. His gang's ambitious docket of robberies ignited the ill will of virtually every upstanding resident of North Texas. The roar grew loud enough that the governor was forced to act, and he called on the always-reliable Texas Rangers, headed by Junius Peak.

After four months of close calls and narrow escapes in which the Sam Bass Gang evaded capture by the Rangers, Bass headed south, intending to make one last major score at a small bank in Round Rock. In the meantime, Jim Murphy, a latecomer to the gang, became friendly with authorities and turned informant. Alerted to Bass's intended target, the Frontier Battalion of Texas—the Rangers—gathered in Round Rock to await the bandits. Among them was Ranger Richard Clayton Ware, who also served as a sheriff and U.S. Marshal.

On July 19, 1878, Ware was lathered up and getting a shave at the local barbershop when Bass and his boys rode into town to buy some tobacco and case the scene of their next heist. As the straight razor scraped Ware's skin, the outlaws hitched their horses in an alley and then walked up the street toward Kopperal's General Store. As they were crossing the dirt road, Travis County deputy sheriff A. W. "High" Grimes observed the men toting six-guns, which was against the law in Round Rock. Not recognizing them as the Sam Bass gang, the deputy approached the sordid cast of cowboys, intending to question them. It would be his last official act.

Bass and his band opened fire on the young deputy, hitting him six times before Grimes fell to the dirt and bled out. The initial gunfire set off a firestorm from the assembled Rangers, as well as local residents, who took up arms to protect their tiny bank. Ware rushed from the barbershop with shaving cream still on his face, pistol in hand, and began firing at the fleeing outlaws. One shot took down Seaborne Barnes. Another hit Sam Bass, although the leader's wounds would later be attributed to another Ranger. Bass staggered to his horse and, amid the gun battle, rode out of town.

The next morning, wary searchers found the legendary outlaw lying against a tree in a field north of Round Rock, mortally wounded but still alive. "I am Sam Bass, the man that has been wanted so long," the wounded gunman said. He also remarked that the lawman who had gunned him down had lather on his face. The Rangers placed the thief on a wagon and drove him back into town to face his judgment. But Bass had other plans. He died in a small shed in Round Rock a day later on July 21, 1878. It was his twenty-seventh birthday.

As one of the most notorious outlaws of the 1870s, Sam Bass has gained near-legendary status as an amiable rogue who robbed from the rich railroads and never gave up a friend. His exploits are inextricably linked to America's Wild West, and in the thirteen decades since his death, his memory has been honored in many mediums and manners. Innumerable books have affectionately referred to Bass as "Robin Hood on a Fast Horse" and "Texas's Beloved Bandit."

The Sam Bass saga has since been fictionalized on radio, television, and film. Streets and businesses bear his name. Frontier festivals have been held in his honor, although, a century after his death, paying tribute to a train robber and cold-blooded killer was deemed politically incorrect. When his postmortem fame spread to the United Kingdom in the late 1800s, Sam Bass's legend even spawned a wax likeness in Madame Tussaud's Waxworks in London.

And so, the legend of Sam Bass—an unschooled roustabout who longed for the romantic West and led a notorious gang in committing Nebraska's greatest train robbery—lives on.

Wild Bill and the McCanles Brothers

He would become the "Prince of Pistoleers," a crack-shot, no-nonsense lawman, able Army scout, Wild West Show performer, and adequate card sharp, but before James Butler Hickok could even become the legendary "Wild Bill," he had to tackle a band of Nebraska outlaws as bad as any in the American West.

Born on May 27, 1837, to William and Polly (Butler) Hickok, James was reared on a small frontier farm a few miles outside of Homer, Illinois. When James's father contracted typhoid fever and became severely ill, his mother helped support the family, providing enough funds to start a small store on the Western frontier. But the store foundered with the financial panic of 1837, just as James was born. With few options, the family turned to farming.

It was a hard life in what was then the Western wilderness of a new nation, but a young James found it invigorating. There were streams to swim and fish, forests to explore, trees to climb, and rabbits, deer, and prairie chickens to hunt. By working on neighboring farms, James earned enough to buy his first firearm, starting a lifelong infatuation with guns. When he wasn't helping out with chores around the farm, James could be found deep in the surrounding forests, tracking game and putting food on his family's table.

On May 5, 1852, William Hickok died. Three of his boys— James, Horace, and Lorenzo—made a go of running the farm for the sake of their mother and sisters, but soon, they all moved to a small house in the quiet village of Homer. For James, accustomed to roaming the woodlands and hunting wild animals and game birds, living in a boring town was like being confined to a prison cell. Enraptured by the stories of Kit Carson and Daniel Boone, James dreamed of heading west. Somehow, his brothers convinced him to stay home for another year to help the family get reestablished.

By 1854, James Hickok had moved to Utica, Illinois, where he found work driving oxen teams on the Illinois and Michigan Canal. The position came to an abrupt end when Hickok threw his boss into the canal for mistreating his team. Historians later speculated that Hickok's action caused him to flee to the West, fearing he would be put in jail for assaulting the abusive employer.

James and his brother, Lorenzo, set out on foot for the Kansas Territory in 1855. The new territory had been opened to homesteaders the year before, and the wide-open farmlands appealed to the Hickoks, who hoped to establish a new venture there. The brothers arrived in St. Louis, Missouri, then a bustling burg overflowing with all types of people, including entrepreneurs, saloon owners, harlots, hunters, traders, and trappers. Lorenzo was overwhelmed by the crowds, and shortly elected to return to Illinois, but not before giving his brother, James, virtually all the money he had to acquire a homestead.

James took passage on a steamboat heading up the Missouri River and disembarked in Kansas, where he wrote to his mother, noting: "I have seen since I have been here sites [sic] that would make the wickedest heartsick . . ." He worked at various jobs, including plowman and scout, and purportedly joined General James Lane's Free State Army by beating out other contenders in a shooting match. For more than a year, James teamed up with a former fur trader named John M. Owen to serve the Free State Army; the two eventually became bodyguards for abolitionist General Lane. Around this time, James began a lifelong friendship with Buffalo Bill Cody.

In his early twenties, the six-foot-tall Hickok was already making a name for himself as a reliable man who remained steady in a crisis. He settled for a time in Monticello, where he was elected town constable and began "proving up" a 160-acre farmstead. James was always eager to move on, however, and in 1858, he gave up the horse and plow and moved to Leavenworth, Kansas. For the next two years, the future Western legend drove stagecoaches and wagons on the Sante Fe Trail for Russell, Majors, and Waddell, a dangerous occupation fraught with backcountry bandits, blinding blizzards, and grizzly bear.

It was during this stint as a teamster that James Butler Hickok purportedly encountered a grizzly bear high on Raton Pass, nearly 8,000 feet in elevation along the Colorado–New Mexico border. While driving his freight wagon through the mountain pass along the Sante Fe Trail in 1860, James stumbled on a cinnamon-colored bear with two cubs in tow. The bear didn't want to give way. Believing he could scare it off, James dismounted from his wagon and approached the bear. Defending its young, the grizzly immediately attacked. In the ensuing battle, James fired several shots into the animal and then drew his knife from its scabbard and fought the beast at close quarters.

When the grizzly finally fell dead on the trail, sliced open by Hickok's knife from its throat to its hindquarters, both warriors were covered in blood. Hickok's shoulder was torn open by the bear's claws, his left arm was essentially crushed, and his cheek was bloodied. Eventually making his way to a town and medical attention, the severely wounded Hickok was sent by the freighting company to Rock Creek Station in Nebraska on light duty, ostensibly to recuperate in the wake of the bear attack. At Rock Creek, Hickok's legend as a capable and deadly gunfighter would begin.

Established just three years before Hickok's arrival on the scene, Rock Creek Station was serving as a rest stop and resupply center for immigrants heading west on the California and Oregon trails. Wagon trains and riders on horseback frequently stopped at the station's makeshift store for hay, grain, flour, sugar, and other provisions.

As the snows melted from the plains in the spring of 1859, about a year before Hickok arrived at Rock Creek, Nebraska Territory, David C. McCanles—a North Carolina native and former sheriff who had left the state with his mistress and a substantial sum of money owed to the county—stopped at the station to rest and stock up. He and his brother, James, were past the halfway point on their long ride to the gold fields of Colorado, where they fully intended to strike it rich. However, when they were greeted by down-and-out miners returning penniless from the same gold camps, the brothers quickly became discouraged about their intended destination.

Opting out of the long ride to the Colorado Rockies and still coveting his stolen stash, the outlaw David McCanles instead bought the Rock Creek Station, built a toll bridge across the creek, and began charging sodbusters and other would-be settlers ten to fifty cents to use the bridge. After building a new

A portrait of David C. McCanles, ca. 1859, taken about two years before the July 12, 1861, gunfight with James Butler Hickok at Rock Creek Station, Nebraska, in which McCanles and two other men died, and the legend of Wild Bill Hickok began. *Photo courtesy of the Nebraska State Historical Society*

cabin and digging a well on the east side of the creek, McCanles established the East Ranch. The following year, Russell, Majors, and Waddell leased the East Ranch from McCanles, where the company operated an Overland Stage stop and, eventually, a Pony Express relay station. McCanles continued to live on and operate the West Ranch.

McCanles, empowered by his business prowess, quickly acquired a reputation for being a bully who was accustomed to getting his way and making threats when he didn't. Historians have since characterized him as a Confederate sympathizer, embezzler, womanizer, outlaw, and genuine rabble-rouser. On several occasions, the entrepreneur sold his toll bridge, only to take it back when the buyers didn't live up to the provisions of their contract.

While Russell, Majors, and Waddell originally had intended to only lease the East Ranch, McCanles convinced them to buy it with one-third down, and the rest paid in monthly installments. The company appointed Horace Wellman as station-keeper, and Hickok soon arrived to assist him with tending stock and other light chores. As spring gave way to summer and the company missed expected payments to McCanles, the scene at the station grew more intense, and would eventually turn deadly.

Ever the intimidating bully, by some accounts McCanles even pestered Hickok unmercifully, chiding him about his girlish figure and feminine features. From the outset, the two never got along. Still miffed over his missed payments, McCanles finally asked Wellman to find out why his company was late in making the agreed-upon compensation for purchase of the East Ranch.

Wellman rode into nearby Brownville to talk to company officials and returned to the station empty-handed on July 11, 1861, only to inform McCanles and Hickok that Russell, Majors, and Waddell was now bankrupt. Incensed, McCanles ordered everyone to leave the East Ranch, began browbeating anyone associated with the venture, and even physically assaulted the aging father of one employee. The next day, matters would come to a head.

On that hot afternoon of July 12, McCanles and his twelve-year-old son, William Monroe, arrived at the East Ranch with two of their employees, James Woods and James Gordon. Demanding immediate settlement or, in the alternative, repossession of the ranch, McCanles delivered his ultimatum in no uncertain terms and with the harshness for which he had become known locally. Wellman, afraid of the belligerent bully, told McCanles he had no authority to return the ranch to his possession.

In the midst of the heated exchange, McCanles reportedly asked for a drink of water. According to noted Hickok biographer, Englishman Joseph G. Rosa, Hickok stepped into the house to get a glass of water for the upset McCanles. When McCanles followed him into the shanty, shots were fired and McCanles stumbled through the door, collapsed, and died.

Other shots rang out, and Woods and Gordon scattered to avoid certain death. Woods was killed just outside the cabin when his skull was smashed by a hoe. Rosa claims, "Gordon fled into the brush, but his escape was thwarted by his own bloodhound, who ran after his master and thus led the killers to him. Gordon was killed with a blast from a shotgun." Young William Monroe ran to his father's side, confirmed his violent death, then stole into the brush and scurried home to report the dreadful news.

Three days later, Hickok, Wellman, and James W. "Doc" Brink, a Pony Express rider, were arrested by lawmen and taken to Beatrice, Nebraska Territory, where they would be tried for the murder of the three men. In turn, each of the three defendants testified that they had been defending company property of the Overland Express. Unimpressed with the evidence presented by the prosecution, Justice of the Peace T. M. Coulter dismissed the charges of murder and released the defendants.

Many local residents regarded the verdict as a sham, and the shoot-out quickly became known as the McCanles Massacre. Despite the initial public outrage, the legend of what occurred at Rock Creek Station quickly grew until the lore had Hickok shooting until he ran out of bullets, then grabbing his knife to finish off the remainder of ten armed attackers who sought to kill him at the Western outpost. Rosa would later write that, "No single gunfight, with the possible exception of the Earp-Clanton fight in October, 1881, in Tombstone, Arizona, has caused so much controversy as the Hickok-McCanles affair at Rock Creek on the afternoon of Friday, July 12, 1861."

Six years later, Colonel George Ward Nichols would immortalize the shoot-out in *Harper's New Monthly Magazine*, albeit with significant embellishment, recounting what he said was the actual story of the McCanles confrontation as told to him by Wild Bill Hickok:

> "You see this M'Kandlas was the Captain of a gang
> of desperadoes, horse thieves, murderers, regular cut-
> throats, who were the terror of everybody on the border,
> and who kept us in the mountains in hot water whenever

they were around. I knew them all in the mountains, where they pretended to be trapping, but they were there hiding from the hangman. M'Kandlas was the biggest scoundrel and bully of them all, and was allers a-braggin' of what he could do. One day I beat him shootin' at a mark, and then threw him at the back-holt. And I didn' [sic] drop him as soft as you would a baby, you may be sure. Well, he got savage mad about it, and swore he would have his revenge on me some time.

"This was just before the war broke out, and we were already takin' sides in the mountains either for the South or the Union. M'Kandlas and his gang were border-ruffians in the Kansas row, and of course they went with the rebs. Bime-by [sic] he clar'd out, and I shouldn't have thought of the feller again if he hadn't crossed my path. It 'pears he didn't forget me.

"It was in '61, when I guided a detachment of cavalry who were comin' in from Camp Floyd. We had nearly reached the Kansas line, and were in South Nebraska, when one afternoon I went out of camp to go to the cabin of an old friend of mine, a Mrs. Waltman. I took only one of my revolvers with me, for although the war had broke out I didn't think it necessary to carry both my pistols, and, in all or'nary scrimmages, one is better than a dozen if you shoot straight. I saw some wild turkeys on the road as I was goin' down, and popped one of 'em over, thinking he'd be just the thing for supper.

"Well, I rode up to Mrs. Waltman's, jumped off my horse, and went into the cabin, which is like most of the cabins on the prarer [sic], with only one room, and that had two doors, one opening in front and t'other on a yard like.

" 'How are you, Mrs. Waltman,' I said, feeling as jolly as you please.

"The minute she saw me she was turned white as a sheet and screamed: 'Is that you, Bill? Oh, God! They will kill you! Run! Run! They will kill you!'

" 'Who's a-goin' to kill me?' I said. 'There's two that can play that game.'

" 'It's M'Kandlas and his gang. There's ten of them, and you've no chance. They've jes' gone down the road to the corn-rack. They came up here only five minutes ago. M'Kandlas was draggin' poor Parson Shipley on the ground with a lariat 'round his neck. The preacher was most dead with choking and the horses stamping on him. M'Kandlas knows yer bringing in that party o' Yankee cavalry, and he swears he'll cut yer heart out. Run, Bill, run! But it's too late; they're coming up the lane.'

"While she was a-talkin', I remembered that I had but one revolver, and a load gone out of that. On the table there was a horn of powder and some little bars of lead. I poured some powder into the empty chamber and rammed the lead after it by hammering the barrel on the table, and had just capped the pistol when I heard M'Kandlas shout: 'There's that d—d Yank Wild Bill's horse; he's here, and we'll skin him alive!'

"If I had thought o' runnin' before, it was too late now, and the house was my best holt—sort of fortress, like. I never thought I should leave the room alive."

The scout stopped his story, rose from his seat, and strode back and forward in a state of great excitement.

"I tell you what it is, Kernel," he resumed, after a while. "I don't mind a scrimmage with these fellers 'round here. Shoot one or two of them and the rest run away. But all of M'Kandlas's gang were reckless, blood-thirsty devils, who would fight as long as they had the strength to pull a trigger. I have been in tight places, but that's one of the few times I said my prayers.

" 'Surround the house and give no quarter!' yelled M'Kandlas. When I heard that I felt as quiet and cool as if I were a-goin' to church. I looked 'round the room and saw a Hawkins rifle hangin' over the bed.

" 'Is that loaded?' said I to Mrs. Waltman.

" 'Yes,' the poor thing whispered. She was so frightened she couldn't speak out loud.

" 'Are you sure?' said I, as I jumped to the bed and caught it from its hooks. Although my eye did not leave the door, yet I could see she nodded 'Yes' again. I put the revolver on the bed, and just then M'Kandlas poked his head inside the doorway, but jumped back when he saw me with the rifle in my hand.

" 'Come on in here, you cowardly dog,' I shouted. 'Come in here, and fight me!'

"M'Kandlas was no coward, if he was a bully. He jumped inside the room with his gun leveled to shoot, but he was not quick enough. My rifle-ball went through his heart. He fell back outside the house, where he was found afterward holding tight to his rifle, which had fallen over his head.

"His disappearance was followed by a yell from his gang, and then there was a dead silence. I put down the rifle and took the revolver, and said to myself: 'Only six shots and nine men to kill. Save your powder, Bill, for the death-hug's a-comin'!' I don't know why it was, Kernel,' continued Bill, looking at me inquiringly, "but at that moment things seemed clear and sharp. I could think strong.

"There was a few seconds of that awful stillness, and then the ruffians came rushing in at both doors. How wild they looked with their red, drunken faces and inflamed eyes, shouting and cussing! But I never aimed more deliberately in my life.

"One—two—three—four; and four men fell dead.

"That didn't stop the rest. Two of them fired their birdguns at me. And then I felt a sting run all over me. The room was full of smoke. Two got in close to me, their eyes glaring out of the clouds. One I knocked down with my fist. 'You are out of the way for a while,' I thought. The second I shot dead. The other three clutched me and crowded me onto the bed. I fought hard. I broke with my hand one man's arm. He had his fingers 'round my throat. Before I could get to my feet I was struck across the breast with the stock of a rifle, and I felt the blood rushing out of my nose and mouth. Then I got ugly, and I remember that I got hold of a knife, and then it was all cloudy like, and I was wild, and I struck savage blows, following the devils up from one side to the other of the room and into the corners, striking and slashing until I knew that every one was dead.

"All of a sudden it seemed as if my heart was on fire. I was bleeding everywhere. I rushed out to the well and drank from the bucket, and then tumbled down in a faint."

Breathless with the intense interest with which I had followed this strange story, all the more thrilling and weird when its hero, seeming to live over again the bloody events of that day, gave way to its terrible spirit with wild, savage gestures. I saw then—what my scrutiny of the morning had failed to discover—the tiger which lay concealed beneath that gentle exterior.

"You must have been hurt almost to death," I said.

"There was eleven buck-shot in me. I carry some of them now. I was cut in thirteen places. All of them had enough to have let the life out of a man. But that blessed old Dr. Mills pulled me safe through it, after a bed siege of many a long week."

Following the incident at Rock Creek Station, Wild Bill Hickok would go on to achieve measurable fame as a Civil War sharpshooter, scout, and spy, and then later as a scout for the U.S. Army in the Western wilderness. He served as a deputy U.S. Marshal, small-town sheriff, and reluctant Wild West Show performer, before drifting into a haze of days filled with saloon banter, gambling, and girls.

In the summer of 1876, the fighting frontier hero, arguably the most famous Western gunfighter of his day, traveled to the booming gold camp of Deadwood, Dakota Territory, where he was shot and killed during a poker game. His assassin, a no-account drifter named "Crooked Nose" Jack McCall, was later hanged. Hickok was buried in Deadwood's Mount Moriah Cemetery.

The Doc Middleton Gang

In a career of cattle rustling and equestrian theft that spanned decades, James "Doc" Middleton Riley earned an unsavory reputation coupled with an unbridled admiration for the thousands of horses he was able to steal in a lifetime of crime on the Nebraska plains.

Variously known as the "Unwickedest Outlaw," a "Robin Hood on Horseback," and "The King of the Horse Thieves," James M. Riley was born in Mississippi on February 9, 1851, as his birth certificate attests, or in Bastrop, Texas, as he later claimed. Although his birthplace may be in question, it's clear he was reared on the flatlands of Texas, where cow punching and horses were a way of life. He purportedly stole his first steed at the age of fourteen, and it took him a long time and several years of special attention in the Nebraska State Prison to break the habit.

His claim of stealing 2,000 horses in two years, the majority owned by Native American tribes and the U.S. Government, would later earn him a spot in Buffalo Bill Cody's Wild West Show, but not before a great many gunshots, a good deal of bloodshed, and a staggering amount of property loss.

While Middleton was his middle name, no one is certain how Riley came to be tabbed "Doc." Some have attributed the sobriquet to his outstanding ability to "doctor" the brands on the cows and horses he stole. Historical records reveal that Doc Middleton was not incredibly attached to his real moniker, and used numerous aliases that included David C. Middleton,

Jack Lyons, Texas Jack, Gold-Tooth Jack, and Gold-Tooth Charley. After all, as an outlaw, there were benefits to not being readily identifiable.

It took Doc just five years to advance from common horse thief to cold-blooded killer. In 1870, at age nineteen, Doc Middleton was convicted of murder in Texas and was sentenced to life in the Huntsville Prison. Four years later, Doc escaped from jail and fled to Nebraska by joining a cattle drive.

Doc kept his head low for the next three years, taking up where he left off before being sent to prison. Unfortunately for him, his time on the lam wouldn't last. In 1877, he was caught stealing horses in Iowa, where he would spend the next year and a half in a Hawkeye state prison. Upon his release, Doc moved to Sidney, Nebraska Territory, where the law hadn't yet arrived. He found easy pickings in the horse herds of the Lakota Sioux tribe, as well as those of the U.S. Government being used by soldiers to fight the Plains Indian wars.

Doc and his "Pony Boys," as they would come to be known, made frequent raids on horse herds held on the Pine Ridge Indian Reservation in extreme southern Dakota Territory, then would run them south to the Sandhills of northern Nebraska Territory, hide out until the heat subsided, and sell the mounts. Among the roughs he assembled for his gang were Jack Nolan, Lee "Curly" Grimes, Kid Wade, and, briefly, Luke Short.

Despite Doc's apparent willingness to use his gun against his fellow man, the leader of the Pony Boys eventually dismissed Curly Grimes for using his firearm in an indiscriminate manner. Grimes would later join another gang robbing stages in the Black Hills, before being gunned down by lawmen while attempting an escape. Meanwhile, Doc and his bad boys made something of a science of stealing horses on the windswept plains.

Doc's prolific thievery resulted in an unintended consequence that eventually would lead the law to focus its attention on bringing his gang's activities to a violent conclusion. Native Americans, upset by the dwindling number of horses in their herds, simply raided ranches in northern Nebraska to replenish their stock. Soon, virtually *all* horse thefts were being attributed to the Pony Boys, and Doc had a $1,000 reward on his head. At about this time, one of his acquaintances said of Doc, "He was a powerful fellow, with a quick, elastic step, and wore a dark sombrero, an overcoat of wildcat skins and a bright handkerchief, and his cowboy make-up gave him the appearance of a typical western frontiersman."

Although he didn't seek public attention, preferring to lie low and cash in on other people's four-legged property, trouble always seemed to find Doc Middleton. Blowing off steam in a Sidney saloon one evening, Doc got into an argument with a soldier from nearby Fort Sidney. The cavalryman, insulted by Doc's fluid tongue, threw a punch that connected with Doc's face, sending him to the floor. When Doc jumped up, the soldier planted another blow that sent the gang leader flying. Calmly, Doc regained his feet, drew his pistol from its holster, and fired a round into the soldier's belly.

By some reports, Doc was quickly arrested by the local sheriff. However, when a lynch mob formed to take care of the offender with decided swiftness, the sheriff purportedly allowed Doc to escape. Doc promptly hopped the first stage out of town.

Already sought by authorities for his horse thefts, the shooting of the soldier now intensified efforts to bring Doc

Middleton and his gang to justice. Unruffled, Doc and his Pony Boys resumed their rustling to such an extent that the Union Pacific Railroad and the Wyoming Stock Growers Association eventually added to the rewards for their capture.

Concerned over repeated horse thefts on the reservation and from government stock, William H. H. Llewellyn, a special agent with the U.S. Department of Justice, was given the sole mission of capturing Doc. Aided by Army soldiers assigned to General George Crook, even this proven man-hunter would have a tricky time meeting the challenge of detaining Nebraska's most infamous outlaw.

Aided by area ranchers he had befriended, and with an unparalleled knowledge of the best hideouts in the Sandhills, Doc was able to evade capture for many months. Eventually, with the promise of a "pardon" signed by the governor of Nebraska Territory, Llewellyn was able to set up a meeting with Doc and his boys in the Niobrara Valley in mid-1879. It was, in fact, a trap to capture the notorious outlaws. In a driving rain, Doc and the Pony Boys rode toward the appointed rendezvous, only to be ambushed as soon as negotiations commenced.

The special agents and their soldiers allegedly fired the first shots with some effect, and the desperadoes quickly returned fire. In the initial barrage of bullets, two of Doc's men fell dead from their horses. Special Agent Hazen, who had accompanied Llewellyn to the meet, was struck in the neck and arm, and suffered a serious wound that entered below his rib cage and exited his back. He would later recover.

Shot in the back (others say the stomach) himself, Doc tumbled from his horse and crawled into some nearby bushes. As the surviving outlaws scurried away from the scene of the skirmish, Doc lay in the mud, attempting to do what he had done best for many years—escape the law. As soldiers and special agents scoured the scene, they stumbled on the wounded Doc Middleton and took him into custody.

Transporting their prisoner first to Sidney, and then on to Cheyenne, Wyoming, authorities would try and convict Doc on a charge of grand larceny. Without much hope of exoneration, some historians contend that the King of the Horse Thieves simply pleaded guilty as charged. Doc was sentenced to five years' incarceration, and, on September 18, 1879, he walked into a cell at the Nebraska State Prison, where he would spend the next three years and nine months.

Released from prison on June 18, 1883, Doc Middleton found that the landscape around him had changed. Law had come to the Western frontier, and with it, all manner of civilized townships, churchgoing folk, and social activities. The vast majority of his old gang had been jailed or killed, and he quickly discovered that he had better adopt a new profession.

Consequently, the thirty-three-year-old ex-convict turned over a new leaf: He got married (for the third time) and began bartending, succeeding in doing what most of his previous associates in crime never accomplished—living nearly thirty more years. Doc settled down with his new, sixteen-year-old wife in Gordon, Nebraska, where he operated a saloon, lived off his reputation, briefly served as a deputy sheriff, and fathered three children. In his spare time, he gambled with limited success.

Historians claim Doc had a softer side that he seldom revealed to outsiders, preferring to maintain his reputation as a gun-toting desperado who would rather steal your horse than let you buy him a drink. One story involving his sentimentality involved a Gordon, Nebraska, girl who fell ill. Although Doc paid the doctor's tab, even the best medical attention of the day couldn't save her, and she died. A shortage of lumber prevented her parents or the local undertaker from providing her with a small coffin to send her to the afterlife. When Doc learned of the dilemma, and the fact that her family intended to bury the little gal wrapped in a shroud, he immediately raced to his bar, tore out a portion of it, and hammered and sawed until he had fashioned her a fitting casket.

Other historians argue that Doc really never did settle down, and actually made a last horse raid to the Pine Ridge Indian Reservation in 1890, taking advantage of the confusion that surrounded the Wounded Knee Massacre. Driving the animals south into familiar Nebraska rangelands, Doc was allegedly caught near the Snake River and jailed, with the horses being returned to the Lakota Sioux.

In late March 1891, a gang of gamblers that supposedly included Doc opened up an illegal gambling den called the White House in Covington, Nebraska, near Sioux City. The venture lasted less than two days when the shooting of former mayor John Peyton, one of the gamblers, cut short the shuffling of cards and the rolling of dice. Doc was said to have suffered a "dangerous wound in the abdomen." A local newspaper explained the sordid incident by concluding: "All were drunk."

The legend of Doc Middleton's exploits didn't end in Nebraska, and, in fact, during the outlaw's heyday, alerts, reports of sightings, and accounts of his thefts were frequently carried in the newspapers of the day, all the way to the East Coast of the U.S. One who admired all the publicity, and, more important, take advantage of it to fuel his own entrepreneurial ventures, was the showman himself—Buffalo Bill Cody. Always looking for a draw for his famed Wild West Show, Buffalo Bill came up with an idea in 1893 that would put Doc Middleton back in the national spotlight.

That year, the World's Columbian Exposition was being conducted in Chicago to memorialize Columbus's discovery of the New World 400 years earlier. Knowing the event would attract huge crowds and sell tickets, Cody sought to bring his Congress of Rough Riders to the Exposition. When his application was denied as not in keeping with the theme of the Exposition, Cody simply leased the land next door to the fairgrounds and commenced building an arena capable of seating 15,000.

On a lark, someone suggested staging a 1,000-mile horseback endurance race as a promotional stunt to generate publicity for the Wild West show. Mentioned over and over, the suggestion was eventually taken seriously. Colonel Cody put up $500 if the race would end in his arena, and the prize purse blossomed to $1,000. Winners also would collect a saddle from Montgomery Ward & Co., a gold-plated, ivory-handled Colt revolver, and other valuable prizes.

Because of his notoriety, and knowing his participation would ensure news coverage, Doc Middleton was asked to compete. The forty-two-year-old ex-con realized he probably couldn't win the competition, but the lure of one more horse race and the chance for national attention and potential future rewards was just too enticing to pass up. As an added benefit, the 1,000-mile cowboy contest would start in Chadron, Nebraska—right in his backyard.

Contestants were allowed two horses each, and could win the race and the $200 first-place prize only by crossing the finish line on one of them. Joining Doc in the race would be eight other riders, including a former stagecoach driver named John Berry, "Rattlesnake Pete" Stephens, teenager "Little Davy" Douglas, and "Indestructible Joe" Gillespie. On the morning of June 13, 1893, with a throng of 4,000 gathered in front of Chadron's Blaine Hotel, a single gunshot sent the nine riders eastward toward Chicago.

In what was pegged as an incredible endurance race that would test the mettle of any man, Little Davy got sick and dropped out before the riders had passed Nebraska's Sandhills. By the time they reached Iowa, Rattlesnake Pete was coughing up blood.

A full two weeks after the nine men had left Chadron on their eastward journey, word arrived at Cody's Chicago showcase that riders were fast approaching. A horde of 10,000 spectators awaited their arrival. In the center of the arena stood Buffalo Bill Cody, bedecked in a stunning white Western outfit highlighted with silver. Beside him were representatives of the Humane Society.

According to historians, Doc Middleton and "Old Joe" Gillespie were the crowd favorites. However, the first rider to stop his sweating mount in front of Colonel Cody was John Berry. The remainder of the riders showed up at the fairgrounds during the ensuing days. Doc, both of whose horses had come up lame, had dropped out in western Illinois. Berry was named winner by Cody and claimed the colonel's cash prize and the saddle, but the rest wasn't that easy. Accusations of cheating were made, the town of Chadron balked at giving its first-place prize to Berry, and instead awarded $200 and the gold-plated revolver to Gillespie. By some accounts, the entire affair ended in a brawl refereed by the Humane Society.

The "King of the Horse Thieves," James "Doc" Middleton Riley, poses with his horse in 1893 following the 1,000-mile race between Chadron, Nebraska, and Chicago. *Photo courtesy of the Nebraska State Historical Society*

For his part in the endurance contest, Middleton was presented with a velvet saddle blanket on which the words CHADRON TO CHICAGO were embroidered. He would treasure it for the rest of his life.

Doc Middleton spent his declining years operating honky-tonks in several Nebraska, South Dakota, and Wyoming towns, with mixed success. He briefly relocated to Edgemont, South Dakota, where he ran a saloon, then traveled to Ardmore, Nebraska, for the same type of venture, though he added bootlegging to his list of criminal pursuits, delivering booze to the Pine Ridge Indian Reservation, where he had once raided thousands of horses. When soldiers from Fort Robinson wrecked his saloon, he packed it in and moved to Orin Junction, an unincorporated community near Douglas, Wyoming, where he ran an illegal saloon under a tent and sold bootleg whiskey and brew.

Doc's final illicit business enterprise tended to attract riffraff of all kinds, including drifters, scammers, and booze hounds. In his early sixties, and worn down by a life spent either on the lam or in prison, Doc was seldom able to quash troubles when they arose. On a cold winter night in December 1913, two drunken customers fought in Doc's illegal saloon, and one ended up with a knife wound. Authorities investigated, charged Doc with operating an illegal bar, and tossed him in the Converse County Jail. He died there, alone, on December 13, 1913, and was buried at county expense two weeks later in the frozen ground of Douglas Park Cemetery.

So ended the life of James "Doc" Middleton Riley—the King of the Horse Thieves—and a Nebraska outlaw legend.

The Demise of Kid Wade

Beginning with his nineteenth year of living, William Albert Wade set himself on a course of infamy that would include horse stealing, hideouts, petty thefts, murder, mayhem, and an early death. His death at the gallows would be undignified. His grave would remain unmarked. But the memory of Kid Wade's exploits lives on in the Sandhills of Nebraska and in the timelessness of modern film.

Wade was indeed just a "kid" when he turned to a life of crime at the age of nineteen. And, for his few remaining years, he would maintain an air of youthful recklessness, coupled with a sharp tongue and a quick gun. With the possible exception of his birth in 1862, little of his formative years is known or documented. Kid Wade's daring deeds began with his adoption into the "Pony Boys" gang of cattle rustlers and horse thieves.

Led by the notorious James M. Riley, aka Doc Middleton, the Pony Boys were the scourge of Nebraska's Niobrara Valley, raiding horseflesh from Dakota Territory's Pine Ridge Indian Reservation and White River region to the ranches scattered throughout northern Nebraska. In Doc, perhaps Kid Wade found the father figure he had never known. By all accounts, Doc took the Kid under his wing much as he would have a son, teaching him the intricacies of horse stealing and hideouts, with the additional skills of gunplay and evading the authorities.

With the Pony Boys operating through much of the 1870s, Kid Wade helped steal thousands of steeds previously owned by the U.S. Government and Lakota Sioux tribes. The outlaws would herd them south to the Sandhills under the cover of darkness, and then hide out in the deep ravines of the Niobrara River. When the "heat" from pursuing posses cooled down, Doc's Pony Boys would simply sell the stock at a discount, pocket the illicit proceeds, and venture into one of northern Nebraska's small towns to hit a saloon, blow off steam, slam a few whiskeys, gamble, and bask in the glow of some sultry saloon girls slinking around, looking for gold pieces.

As the youngster in the gang, Kid Wade was eager to prove himself to his older compatriots. This often led to a hastily drawn gun, belittling of crime victims and others less powerful, and a complete lack of conscience or moral courage. Variously described as appearing to be a cross between a bum and a cat burglar, Kid was of average height and a bit bowlegged, no doubt due to extended periods in the saddle. His jutting jaw wouldn't accommodate a beard, adding to his youthful appearance and his victims' predisposition toward underestimating his ruthlessness.

Kid Wade never held a legitimate job, relying instead on his stealth, his six-gun, and his lust for obtaining that which he did not own to see him through the world. And, with a dearth of lawmen along the Western frontier in which the Pony Boys operated, Kid Wade would enjoy the "easy pickings" of northern Nebraska Territory for several years.

But it would not always be thus. Drawn by homestead acts and well-watered virgin prairies that stretched to the horizon, sodbusters and would-be cattle kings were flocking to the wide-open Nebraska Territory throughout the 1870s and '80s, and they brought their own form of law with them.

Pioneers began settling the town of Ainsworth in 1880, just a few miles south of the Niobrara River in north-central Nebraska.

As was the case with so many towns settled along a freighting trail on the open prairie, among Ainsworth's earliest businesses were a general store, an elevator for grain storage, a hotel, bank, restaurant, hardware store, and livery, soon followed by lawyers, doctors, real estate agents, and newspaper publishers.

Ainsworth was incorporated on December 11, 1883, soon after the county had been established, and residents were intent on making the town a center of commerce for northern Nebraska. The following year, the new Congregational Church opened and the town held its first fair on Nannie Osborn's claim southwest of town. Glen Nesbit won the prize as prettiest baby, and Millie Cheney received a gold thimble for being the most accomplished young lady in the county.

Despite the advancements toward establishing a civilized town of upstanding, God-fearing citizens, the lawless West nevertheless surrounded them. Native American tribes were still fighting to maintain their nomadic existence on the Plains, and gangs of hooligans, stage robbers, crooks, culprits, and cut-throats passed through on horseback in the night, occasionally with posses in pursuit.

Doc Middleton's Pony Boys, with Kid Wade in tow, were among the most celebrated and, simultaneously, the most despised of the desperadoes who would rob anything, from the "gold coaches" of the Black Hills, Dakota Territory, to the cattle herds of Texas. Favoring government and Indian ponies, the fugitives commanded a bounty as large as $1,000 each for their capture, and when the law came calling, the Pony Boys' favorite hideout was the Sandhills, where some even claimed they maintained an underground lair for extended stays.

While some local ranchers initially tolerated the raids of the Pony Boys—frankly, because they were "only stealing Indian horses"—the Natives were understandably less broad-minded. When members of the tribes reciprocated and began replenishing their stock with horses culled from area ranches, virtually every horse theft was tied to the Pony Boys' activities. Soon, the Union Pacific, the Stock Growers Association, and the U.S. Government had agents, marshals, and bounty hunters alerted to the lucrative rewards posted on the heads of Doc Middleton, Kid Wade, and their band of rustlers.

It is likely that Kid Wade was with Doc Middleton in mid-1879 when the outlaw legend agreed to meet Special Agent William H. H. Llewellyn of the U.S. Department of Justice to discuss a potential pardon for the gang. When the lawmen staged an ambush and opened fire, two of the outlaws were shot from their saddles, while Doc was wounded and captured. Kid Wade escaped to the refuge of the Sandhills, while a Cheyenne, Wyoming, court sentenced his former boss to five years in a Nebraska prison.

Though accounts are rare, Kid Wade purportedly assembled his own gang and continued raiding horse herds and robbing stagecoaches, drinking and gambling the proceeds, and generally taking up where his old gang had left off. But Kid Wade's style was less cautious than that of Doc Middleton, and soon the same lawmen that had pursued Doc set their sights on Kid Wade and his brazen bandits. Time and again, Kid and his gang of ruffians slipped through the cordon set by rangers and special agents.

Frustrated by the lack of law enforcement in northern Nebraska, the limited success of marshals in bringing hooligans to justice, and tired of losing bank deposits, stage cargo, live-stock, and horses to the illegal activities of the outlaws, towns-people and area ranchers took up arms to defend their families, their property, and their towns. In the fall of 1883, these hardy pioneers established the Niobrara Mutual Protection Association, ostensibly to protect their herds. Other vigilante groups formed throughout the Niobrara Valley.

According to Nebraska historian and author, Harold Hutton, "These extra-legal lawmen did not always operate in secrecy, but surfaced in the form of 'posses' in pursuit of rustlers, or the vigilantes openly cooperated with the sheriffs. These county officers apparently welcomed the assistance of the regulators. Although the vigilantes became inactive in the late 1890s, rustlers continued to raid stock pens along the Niobrara River as late as 1906."

Operating near the Niobrara River in the 1880s, Kid Wade would stop for supplies and liquor in towns such as Ainsworth and nearby Bassett, a small farming community a few miles to the east. Kid Wade's gang supposedly conducted raids and robberies from the Black Hills to western Iowa. It was in Iowa where the "regulators"—really, self-styled vigilantes—nabbed Kid Wade.

Wade had earlier escaped from prison, no doubt sentenced for stealing horses. The vigilantes followed his gang's trail to Iowa and took him into custody on January 24, 1884. When the Kid realized that other members of his gang were turning on him and implicating him in assorted crimes in an attempt to save themselves, he, too, began singing like a canary, and, in the process, implicated himself.

Likely passed westward by cooperating "mutual protection associations," on his way to trial in Ainsworth, the vigilantes

While no photograph of William Albert "Kid" Wade is known to exist, this float was built in August 1939, to commemorate the hanging of Kid Wade in Bassett, Nebraska, a half-century earlier. *Photo courtesy of the Nebraska State Historical Society*

stopped in Bassett for the night, where they conducted a public hearing so local residents could make their own determination about Kid Wade's guilt, and his treatment as a prisoner of the regulators.

"I've been well treated," the Kid told local residents, by one account. "I'm here of my own free will. I've not been threatened or offered leniency." The Kid also said he had no knowledge of any band of horse thieves, though he intimated that several local townspeople of some standing were involved in the ongoing thefts.

That night, Holt County law officers took him into custody and deposited their prisoner under guard at the Bassett Hotel. As was his custom, Kid Wade spread a blanket on the floor and bedded down for the evening. It would be a short night.

Sometime in the early morning hours of February 8, 1884, a dozen masked vigilantes stormed the hotel at gunpoint, dismissed the guard, and took Kid Wade from his room.

"Please don't hang me," twenty-two-year-old Kid Wade begged. "I'll never steal another horse again."

The next morning, the body of Kid Wade was found swinging freely from a stout rope attached to a railroad whistling post 1 mile east of Bassett. A few days later, William Albert "Kid" Wade was laid to rest in a plain pine box on Bassett Hill. A few months later, the Brown County Commission agreed to pay the local undertaker for the $20 coffin.

Though Kid Wade had led a life shortened by his own misdeeds, and, in fact, had played the role of an outlaw for a mere three years, the legend and lore of his exploits have endured for more than a century.

In 2007, Aussie actor Russell Crowe played Kid Wade in the blockbuster film, *3:10 to Yuma*. Many liberties were taken with the facts surrounding Kid Wade's real life on the run, his young age, and his eventual demise. But one line, uttered by Crowe in the midst of the modern-day Western, stood out as indicative of the real life of a real Nebraska outlaw legend.

Citing Proverbs 13:3, Crowe said, "He that keepeth his mouth, keepeth his life. He that opens his lips too wide shall bring on his own destruction."

Flatnose Currie and the Wild Bunch

The career of crime attributed to George Sutherland "Flatnose" Currie began and ended in Nebraska. Between those bookends in the Cornhusker State, Flatnose Currie was involved in innumerable horse thefts, cattle rustling, bank heists, train robberies, and the murders of several lawmen charged with bringing him and his associates to justice.

As a member of the notorious Wild Bunch, whose members also included Butch Cassidy, the Sundance Kid, and a quick-tempered killer known as Kid Curry, Flatnose Currie led a life on the lam, hiding out in places that ranged from Nebraska's Sandhills and Wyoming's Hole in the Wall to Utah's Robbers Roost, Montana's Hi-Line, and, by some accounts, as far south as Bolivia.

Born on Canada's Prince Edward Island around 1864, accounts of Flatnose Currie's early life are relatively unknown. At some point in his youth, he moved with his family to the vast expanses of Nebraska Territory, where his parents settled near the small ranching community of Chadron. Nearing manhood, Currie allegedly found the work of rustling cattle and horses from neighbor's ranches far preferable to the backbreaking labor it took to establish a homestead and "prove up" the land, as so many settlers were then doing.

At one point in his colorful career, which entailed the repetitive theft of horses not under his ownership, one of the equines apparently kicked George in the face, producing his signature feature. At various times, he was known as "Big Nose" and "Flatnose" Currie, a sobriquet that would catch on with the legions of lawmen who sought to apprehend him over the ensuing years, making the bandit readily identifiable.

The misdeeds attributed to Flatnose Currie have long been mixed in history with those actually performed by a mean and menacing man named Harvey Logan, who may have been Flatnose's nephew. Shortly after forming the Wild Bunch and, in testament to his admiration for Flatnose Currie, Logan would adopt his name and become known as Kid Curry.

To further the confusion, Kid Curry's brothers—Lonny and Johnny Logan—also adopted Curry as a surname and ran rampant with the Wild Bunch. After Kid Curry's quick and remorseless gunplay left at least two lawmen dead, he would be widely regarded by authorities as one of the most dangerous and unpredictable men to ever roam the Wild West.

Flatnose Currie, however, started his career of crime on a softer note. He began his illustrious march into the annals of Nebraska outlaw lore by rustling cows and stealing horses from ranches, reservations, and even the U.S. Government, which maintained herds of ponies at numerous forts through-out the West. Among them was Fort Robinson, some 30 miles southwest of his childhood home in Chadron. The Pine Ridge Indian Reservation and its large herds of stock were found to the northeast, just over the border in Dakota Territory. Fol-lowing in the footsteps of other thieves who had practiced the same vocation for two decades before Flatnose arrived on the scene, he and his associates would hide out in the rolling hills, canyons, and forests of the Sandhills.

51

However, by the late 1880s and early '90s, lawmen were becoming as familiar with the Sandhills as the outlaws. Consequently, when the law came too close once too often, Flatnose and his band headed west into the lonesome country of eastern Wyoming. They settled at a then-little-known sanctuary known as the Hole in the Wall near present-day Sundance, in extreme northeastern Wyoming. Over the next several years the bandits made frequent forays into the Dakotas, Montana, Utah, and Colorado to rob trains, banks, stages, and the occasional unlucky rancher. Then, they would take their loot and hightail it to the hinterlands of eastern Wyoming, still among the least populated places in the U.S.

It was during one of Flatnose Currie's extended stays at the Hole in the Wall that he met and befriended Harvey, Lonny, and Johnny Logan. As a measure of respect for their uncle, each of the Logans adopted Flatnose's last name, although historians have traditionally spelled them with slight variations. Nonetheless, by many accounts, Flatnose was a man who commanded respect.

One longtime friend of Flatnose Currie, who some knew as Geo Carver, would later remark that most of his close friends and associates in crime called Flatnose "Colonel, because he was such a large, well-proportioned man, with a military appearance, straight as an arrow and strong as a horse."

The sheer, crimson canyon wall featured a "hole" or gash through which rustlers could herd their stolen cattle and horses away from the prying eyes of the law. Sentries stationed on top of the sandstone outcroppings could see posses or other riders approaching from miles away, allowing ample time to send warning to those outlaws who were hiding in ramshackle cabins scattered near the Hole in the Wall.

In her new and well-researched biography of the Sundance Kid, author and historian Donna B. Ernst retraces the Outlaw Trail, which was comprised of a series of hideouts and safe houses throughout the Old West. The Wild Bunch, as the gang was known, would become one of the best-known groups of bandits to ever roam the West, earning the moniker by shooting up saloons and main streets as easily as they raided trains and banks.

According to Ernst, the Wild Bunch had "a loose membership of about twenty-five men, but any given robbery seldom involved more than two or three of the same men from any previous or future holdup." The core group consisted of five men: the leader, Robert LeRoy Parker, alias Butch Cassidy; Harvey Alexander Logan, alias Kid Curry (who would murder nine men); Benjamin Arnold Kilpatrick, known as the Tall Texan; William Richard Carver, alias Will Causey; and Harry Alonzo Longabaugh, known forever after as the Sundance Kid.

When Kid Curry arrived at the outlaw outpost in the 1890s, Flatnose had been content with spending his days stealing cows and horses—easy pickings in the Old West. But the Kid's influence, coupled with that of newcomers Butch Cassidy and the Sundance Kid, soon had Flatnose eyeing the cash stashed in the vaults of the region's banks.

As Currie and his gang advanced from rustling to robbing, all conducted with a distinctive flair that included the liberal use of firearms and dynamite, they became the Wild Bunch. Following lucrative raids and robberies, and during the winter months, the bandits hid out in the Hole in the Wall until law enforcement officers raided it in 1897. In the off-season, the outlaws frequently took legitimate work at area ranches, where local residents were keenly aware of their nefarious activities but tolerated the Wild Bunch, as long as they didn't foul their own nest. Other hideouts used by the gang included Robbers Roost in the high desert canyons of Utah; Powder Springs, in extreme southwestern Wyoming; and the Hi-Line of Montana, near the present-day towns of Malta and Culbertson, just south of the Canadian border.

By 1897, the Wild Bunch was experienced enough to take their game to a whole new level. Flatnose Currie and the Wild Bunch set their sights on the big bank in Belle Fourche, a sheep, cattle, and commerce hub on the northern fringe of South Dakota's Black Hills. The town had been destroyed by a major conflagration in late September 1895, but just two summers later, the bustling community had been rebuilt, and was ready to roll out the red carpet for a reunion of Civil War soldiers. The affair promised to be one of the major celebrations of the year.

Flatnose Currie and his gang had learned of the impending festivities and had decided it would provide an opportune time to relieve the Butte County Bank of its excess currency. Located in the town center, where the Civil War reunion was taking place, Flatnose surmised that all the bank deposits would swell the bank's coffers, while the strange faces in town would provide the ideal cover for their illicit activities. They headed toward Belle Fourche, today located just a few miles from the geographic center of the U.S.

Accompanied by brothers Harvey and Lonny Logan, Tom O'Day, and Walt Punteney, Flatnose camped just outside of Belle Fourche during the weekend celebration. On Monday morning, June 28, 1897, Flatnose sent O'Day into town to reconnoiter. But O'Day promptly forgot his assignment, stopped at a downtown saloon, and got liquored up with a bunch of newfound friends. When he didn't return, Flatnose elected to proceed with the planned robbery anyway.

As the town clock struck 10:00 a.m., the remaining four outlaws hitched up their horses near the bank and walked in the front door. Flatnose and company ordered the two bank employees and five customers in the lobby to reach for the sky. As they did, a hardware store owner across the street happened to notice their actions, and slowly walked onto the boardwalk for a closer look. Just then, O'Day, who had by then remembered his assignment, came sauntering up Sixth Street, noticed the merchant eyeing the bank, pulled his six-gun, and fired several rounds at the fleeing busybody.

Alerted to the robbery by the gunfire, the townspeople took up arms. The hostages in the bank took advantage of their startled captors and fled outside. Head cashier Arthur Marble scooped up a revolver from behind the counter and fired a couple rounds at the now-fleeing bank robbers. When O'Day's horse, spooked by the gunshots, ran away, the still-tipsy outlaw hopped on a mule that elected not to work that day. Frantically hustling to an outhouse located between Sebastian's Saloon and the *Times* printing office, O'Day sought to discard his weapon. But an alert butcher named Rusaw Bowman watched O'Day enter the outhouse and took him into custody at gunpoint when he left the latrine. The suspect's handgun was retrieved with a rake, and bullets were discovered on his person, along with nearly $400 in cash and a pint of whiskey.

Unfortunately, another drunk had burned down the town's jail at the onset of the Civil War festivities two days earlier, so the marshal simply locked O'Day in the same bank vault his friends had attempted to rob earlier that day. The suspect was transferred to Deadwood the next day, where he was held in the Lawrence County Jail pending trial.

Meanwhile, Flatnose Currie and his three compatriots headed southwest into the familiar territory of Wyoming. Once they had crossed the state line, Flatnose and Lonny Logan headed for their refuge at the Hole in the Wall, while Harvey Logan and Punteney rode for Powder Springs, a hideout on the border with Utah. Since the bandits were successful in their escape, the holdup at the Belle Fourche bank would become larger than life. In fact, the outlaws probably garnered only $97 grabbed from a bank customer's hand as they were heading out the door.

Nonetheless, Pinkertons and law officers traced Flatnose Currie, Butch Cassidy, and the Sundance Kid, as well as several of their known associates, for the next several years. Innumerable train robberies, bank holdups, and the like were attributed to the Wild Bunch, although it is doubtful even these prolific criminals could have staged so many crimes.

In the early morning hours of July 14, 1898, a Southern Pacific passenger train was leaving Humboldt, Nevada, when two outlaws jumped on board the tender car and pulled six-shooters on the train's engineer and fireman, ordering them to stop the train. Met by a third outlaw in waiting, the three desperadoes ordered the trainmen to open the express car door. When the express messenger refused, the outlaws struck a match and lit a stick of dynamite, which exploded at the rear door to the express car. Warned that the next blast would kill him and destroy the train car, the express messenger slowly opened the door to the waiting outlaws, who stormed inside.

A second dynamite blast opened the safe, blew the roof off the express car, and devastated its interior.

In addition to a few pieces of jewelry, the bandits carted off $26,000 in currency and coin. For this and other alleged robberies, Flatnose Currie and his friends soon had a $1,000 price on their heads. When a small saloon in Elko, Nevada, was robbed about a year later, the deed was attributed to Flatnose, Sundance, and Kid Curry. And, when three men held up the bank in Winnemucca, Nevada, eighteen months later, the same trio was named as suspects.

Although not the first time, the use of dynamite in the commission of the train heist attracted national attention, and put the outlaws' names before a public eager to know everything that happened on the Western frontier. When the Wild Bunch struck the Union Pacific's Overland Flyer at Wilcox, Wyoming, less than a year after the Southern Pacific train robbery, their fame was assured.

This latest exploit began shortly after 2:00 a.m. June 2, 1899, as the Union Pacific's Overland Flyer was chugging down the tracks near Rock Creek, Wyoming, a tiny railroad town servicing the needs of area ranchers as well as the federal government at nearby Fort Fetterman. When two men were seen standing in a driving rain, waving a lantern along the side of the tracks, the train's engineer feared an approaching bridge may have washed out, and he hit the skids. When the train finally halted, two masked men forced their way on board at gunpoint and ordered the engineer to proceed with all haste past the bridge up ahead.

When the engineer hesitated, one of the crooks pistol-whipped him with his Colt revolver. What the engineer could not have known was that the outlaws had already set and lit dynamite charges on the trestle to prevent any posses from pursuing them via a similar mode of transport. Just as the train cleared the trestle and stopped, an explosion rocked the locomotive. After disconnecting the passenger cars from the steam engine, express, baggage, and mail cars, the train proceeded up the tracks for a couple of miles, where four more bandits were waiting.

With practiced patience, the robbers used the next two hours and a healthy supply of dynamite to blow the doors off the express and mail cars before blasting open the safe. However, unschooled in the appropriate use of dynamite, the outlaws set a heavy charge on the substantial vault, which succeeded in getting it open but, as an unintended consequence, also blew the roof off the train car and obliterated its sides.

Bolstered by their haul of $50,000 in cash, gold coin, unsigned bank notes, and jewelry that included four exceptional Elgin watches, the outlaws scattered for the hinterlands.

The Union Pacific immediately offered a reward of $1,000 each for their capture, dead or alive, and the federal government and the Pacific Express Company, which owned the safe, matched the reward. Posses formed, boarded specially outfitted train cars capable of accommodating them and their mounts, and arrived at the scene of the crime seven hours after it had occurred. Wyoming governor DeForest Richards called out the state militia, and by the time the Pinkerton Detective Agency and the Burlington Railroad added their agents, more than 100 gun-toting, reward-hungry men were pursuing the culprits.

The Wild Bunch was immediately suspected of staging the holdup, and, when several of the train's crewmen described one of the bandits as five-foot-nine, 185 pounds, with blue eyes and "a peculiar nose, flattened at the bridge," authorities matched that with the likeness of George Sutherland "Flatnose" Currie.

The outlaws had planned in advance for their getaway, posting fresh mounts along their escape route to allow them to stay ahead of the posse. But a rancher near Horse Ranch, Wyoming, saw the thieves and reported the sighting to authorities in Casper. Sheriff Josiah Hazen and his posse caught up to the crooks and a brief gunfight ensued, wounding only a few ponies, before the outlaws fled further north.

Hiding beneath a rock ledge on Teapot Creek three days after the train robbery, and believing they had evaded the posse, Flatnose, Kid Curry, and the Sundance Kid were catching some rest when the posse stumbled onto their hideaway. In the hail of gunfire that soon erupted, Sheriff Hazen was hit by a shot fired by Kid Curry, a wound from which he would soon die. Taking advantage of the posse leader's mortal wound and heavy rains that began to fall, the outlaws escaped up the creek on foot, losing a portion of their loot in the swollen stream. The only thing the posse captured was a few of the outlaws' horses, left tethered in a nearby canyon.

Meanwhile, Flatnose, Curry, and Sundance "borrowed" a few horses from a nearby ranch and headed for their Hole in the Wall hideout. Encountering a lone deputy sheriff, William Dean, near the north fork of the Powder River, Kid Curry dispatched him with a gunshot just as he had Sheriff Hazen.

Eight months later, Lonny Logan (Curry) was shot and killed by Pinkerton agents as he attempted to flee his aunt's home in Kansas. In August 1900, the Wild Bunch, sans Flatnose Currie, struck the Union Pacific train near Tipton, Wyoming, using dynamite to blow the safe and riding away with $55,000 in cash and jewelry. Two weeks later, members of the same gang, led by Butch Cassidy and the Sundance Kid, robbed the bank in Winnemucca, Nevada, nabbing more than $32,000, including $31,000 in gold coins. When one of the bank bags containing the loot broke open during the escape, the thieves scooped up what they could, but purportedly left $6,000 to $7,000 in $20 gold pieces scattered in the street.

With an ample stake, Butch Cassidy and the Sundance Kid fled the West, stopping over in Fort Worth and New York City before boarding a steamer headed for Buenos Aires, Argentina, and their South American adventure. Some say other members of the Wild Bunch, including Flatnose Currie, accompanied the Western legends. However, a photo of the Hole in the Wall Gang taken in November 1900, in Fort Worth, Texas, doesn't include Flatnose. In fact, Butch Cassidy and the Sundance Kid would settle for a time and attempt ranching in Argentina. But their past eventually caught up with them, and, wrongly accused of robbing a bank, they in turn did stage a series of robberies. In 1906, they were working as payroll guards for the Concordia Mines near La Paz, Bolivia.

But the legitimate work wouldn't last. On November 4, 1908, Butch and Sundance robbed two payroll guards of 80,000 pesos, roughly $100,000 today. Two days later they were cornered by militia in a San Vicente, Bolivia, home, and it was here that their days as the most-revered Western outlaws would end. After exchanging gunfire with the troops, the nighttime scene grew silent. The next morning, an officer entered the house to find both men dead. An inquest in the ensuing days would find that, with no escape, Butch had apparently shot Sundance, and then turned the gun on himself. The duo's

George Sutherland "Flatnose" Currie led a life of crime with Butch Cassidy and the Sundance Kid's Wild Bunch. His death at the hands of lawmen was reported several times, even though some historians contend he lived out the latter years of his life with a daughter in Chadron, Nebraska, where this headstone sits in the Greenwood Cemetery. *Photo by T. D. Griffith*

exploits would be immortalized nearly six decades later in the classic Western film, *Butch Cassidy and the Sundance Kid*, starring Robert Redford and Paul Newman.

Meanwhile, the sands of time covered the outlaw trail of George Flatnose Currie. Some reports had him shot by lawman Jessie M. Tyler in April 1900, as the outlaw was rustling cattle in Grand County, Utah. Kid Curry allegedly avenged his uncle's death and that of his brother, Lonny, by riding to Utah and gunning down Sheriff Tyler and his deputy, Sam Jenkins. Kid Curry was imprisoned in the early 1900s, escaped from jail in June 1903, and then maintained tradition by robbing a train in Parachute, Colorado, a few weeks later. When a pursuing posse wounded the desperado, he elected not to return to jail and took the easy way out, putting a bullet in his own head.

But Flatnose Currie, who had begun his career of crime on the Nebraska Panhandle, purportedly returned to his home range and lived out his life with his daughter.

Charles Wesley Cox and Goldie Williams

As an outlaw, Charles Wesley Cox was quite successful, committing crimes, avoiding posses that once grew to as many as 10,000 men, and evading the law for more than a quarter-century. As a man, Charles Wesley Cox was despicable, carrying out crimes as heinous and horrible as any of his outlaw predecessors could have imagined.

The Nebraska of 1912 was similar to many other Midwestern states of the era, with too little rain when the crops needed it, not enough grass for the cattle, and a burgeoning population that threatened to take over every quarter-section of ground in this once sparsely settled state. When the Civil War began a half-century before, Nebraska Territory had less than 29,000 residents. Now, in the new century, bolstered by exceptional farm- and ranchlands, wide-open spaces, and fast-growing cities, Nebraska had grown to over a million inhabitants.

Early in the year, British explorer Robert F. Scott led an expedition to the Antarctic, reaching the South Pole on January 17, 1912, only to learn that they had been beaten to the punch by Norwegian Roald Amundsen. During their fateful return trip, Scott and the four other members of his Discovery Expedition perished from a lethal combination of exhaustion, starvation, and hypothermia.

Then on April 14, the unimaginable happened when the unsinkable steamship RMS *Titanic* hit an iceberg on its maiden voyage across the Atlantic from Southampton, England, to New York City. The collision tore a gash along a quarter of the ship, sending the $7.5 million ocean liner to a dark grave on the sea bottom, along with 1,503 passengers and crew.

Later in 1912, New Mexico and Arizona became the forty-seventh and forty-eighth states, respectively, admitted to the Union.

Closer to home, a major tornado struck Nebraska on June 12, 1912, destroying farmhouses near the town of Hallam in the extreme southeastern part of the state, leveling barns and out-buildings, and killing a large number of livestock. According to the *Lincoln Daily News*, residents were able to save themselves only by taking refuge in their root cellars.

Meanwhile, 100 miles to the west, in the tiny settlement of Grand Island, Nebraska, townspeople were going about their day, servicing area farmers who were preparing to plant their sugar beets on the fertile croplands that bordered the North Platte River. The settlement had been established in 1857 by thirty-five German immigrants, and the Union Pacific Rail-road's arrival in 1873 had ensured the community's survival, if not its prosperity. By 1905, the town was bustling with pioneer activity. That same year, Henry Fonda, who would become one of America's most revered motion picture stars, was born in Grand Island.

But heartache was destined to come to the heartland. As it had for the past century, Middle America was attracting travel-ers of a different ilk, captivated by the call of the West and all the dreams it entailed, but not really willing to work as hard as the prosperous farmers around them to achieve that dream. Such was one Charles Wesley Cox, an occasional laborer when he felt like working, which occurred only sporadically—for Cox often became fixated on his perverse pleasures, and those inevitably involved young children.

On a mild February afternoon during the winter of 1912, Cox's primal desires and his inability to resist satisfying them would forever change the way the residents of Grand Island and, perhaps, all of Nebraska, perceived strangers and the incomprehensible ways of the outside world.

On February 6, 1912, Cox found that he had a new friend in the form of one ten-year-old girl, Goldie Williams. Young and energetic and full of questions, Goldie was generally unaware of the devious nature of man and, specifically, of the demented cravings of the thirty-six-year-old Cox.

Promising his young friend a new pair of skates, Cox lured Goldie to a vacant house on Grand Island's northeast side. The place was unoccupied only because it was new, and still under construction. Tools, equipment, and supplies still littered the inside of the house, where workmen had been putting the finishing touches on the new residence.

Cox and Goldie probably had a quick look around the home's interior before things took a startling twist. There, on that gray Tuesday afternoon in the middle of Nebraska, Charles Wesley Cox attacked the ten-year-old girl he had befriended. He raped her, beat her to death, and, finally, in one last act of depravity, covered her small, lifeless body with quicklime before making his escape.

While the young girl's body lay in the stillness of that quiet house, Cox calmly made his way through town, stopped at his employer's place to retrieve his last paycheck, and put Grand Island in his past as quickly as humanly possible.

Later that evening, Goldie Williams's parents noticed her absence and began to look around for her. After all, a missing child in a place where neighborhoods were filled with children and people didn't lock their doors was nothing unusual. But as the hours passed and the night grew darker, the Williamses realized their daughter was gone.

By morning, police had been alerted, searchers had been assembled, and volunteers were flocking to every neighborhood in Grand Island, all on the lookout for ten-year-old Goldie. Authorities and volunteers spent the entire day of February 7 knocking on doors, looking in vehicles, and asking questions. By that evening, more than twenty-four hours after the girl's disappearance, everyone was growing frantic. Police rousted transients near the railroad, expanded their dragnet, and brought an increasingly hard edge to their questions.

Having covered every nook and cranny of Grand Island by Thursday morning, volunteers were directed by authorities to examine it all over again, with closer attention to detail. Walking past the new house under construction in northeast Grand Island, and not knowing whether anyone had thought to go inside, volunteer searcher William Ned decided to give it a closer look.

Making his way inside, Ned likely could see tools and equipment scattered about. He canvassed the small rooms of the house, listening for any telltale sign that the girl was alive while paying close attention to the closets and other places where a body might be hidden. Ned was about to complete his search and exit the house when he noticed a door lying on its face. When he lifted it, Ned immediately knew he had found the girl for whom the entire town was searching. There, beneath the unfinished wooden door, was little Goldie Williams, a Grand Islander who would not celebrate her eleventh birthday.

News of the discovery of Goldie Williams's body sent a collective shiver through the close-knit town, and authorities quickly realized their search for the young schoolgirl would now evolve into a relentless hunt for the man who had committed an atrocity.

The next morning, the *Weekly News-Journal* in Norfolk, Nebraska, blared in a front-page headline, GRAND ISLAND CHILD'S RAVISHED BODY FOUND, sending shock waves throughout the civilized societies of the whole state. Subheadings carried the ghastly highlights of the case, including, "Dead Body of 10-Year-Old Goldie Williams Recovered," "Murdered by Man of 40 Years," "Little Body, Bruised and Mutilated, Is Hidden," and "Killed Her with a Club."

While the story did not carry a great deal of new information, it did begin and end with an eerie prediction that may have been regarded by anyone associated with the crime as an unveiled threat.

In bold-faced type, as a lead-in to the newspaper article, was printed, "No Trace of the Man, Who Was a Stranger in Grand Island, Has Been Found—He Will Be Lynched if Posses Now Hunting Can Find Him." The *Weekly News-Journal* reported:

> The dead body of little Goldie Williams, 10 years old, was found at noon today in a vacant house in the northeast part of town. It was covered with quicklime, a quantity of which was in the house, and further hidden by a door which had been thrown over it.
>
> Authorities do not expect to prevent lynching should the assailant be captured.

Little Body Had Been Mutilated.

The little girl disappeared Tuesday evening about 5 o'clock in company with a man about 40 years old, who was a stranger here. When her body was found, it was horribly mutilated and had been ravished.

Her captor had caused her death by blows from his fist, her face showing the marks of a horrible beating.

The body was discovered by William Ned, one of the searchers. The house in which he found it was not searched yesterday because it was newly constructed and no one thought of the little girl being hidden there. The search was this noon transformed from one for the girl and her captor to one for the captor alone, but it had not abated in thoroughness or zeal.

Lynch Him if He's Caught.

Yesterday the town was canvassed from house to house. Today posses are making a hunt through the surrounding country, looking in every farm house and outbuilding.

All day and last night from the time the fire bell brought out the citizens to join in the hunt, hundreds of people have been patrolling the vicinity. It is believed certain that a lynching will follow if the murderer is caught.

Mute Evidence of Death Struggle.

The little girl's body was found at 4 o'clock this afternoon. A 2x4 club covered with blood and with some of the little girl's hair matted to it, told mutely of the desperate death struggle made by the child against the rapist.

The little girl disappeared with the stranger Tuesday afternoon. She was lured away with him on promise of a pair of skates. They were last seen that night at 8 o'clock.

The child's parents are poor, but nothing will be left undone to apprehend the murderer. A big reward is being collected. The great excitement of yesterday is only intensified this afternoon.

In the same edition of the *Weekly News-Journal*, it was reported that Nebraska governor Chester H. Aldrich, when informed of the gruesome murder, pledged a $200 reward for the apprehension of the person responsible for the crime. "Yes, sir, I will offer a reward for the man who killed that little girl," Governor Aldrich, in Norfolk that Thursday afternoon, told the *News-Journal.* "You can say that I will offer a reward of $200 as provided by the statutes of the state, and I will make it official when I get back to Lincoln. The state of Nebraska will exhaust every means to run this criminal down and nothing will be left undone."

And that's exactly what they did. In a matter of hours, virtually every able-bodied man within 60 miles of Grand Island had checked the load in his shotgun, grabbed a few extra shells, donned a coat, and taken up the search for the most-despised outlaw thus far in Nebraska history.

Authorities followed up on myriad leads. On February 10, four days after the murder, the Associated Press reported that the second arrest of a possible suspect in the murder had occurred that morning, "when a stranger was taken in town and thoroughly questioned by Police Judge Kroeger, Chief Arbogast and Sheriff Sievers. The man, however, did not answer the description, nor was there any evidence justifying his retention further than that he was a stranger and that his unusual actions had attracted attention to him."

Furthermore, the AP noted: "The coroner's jury, which was convened at a late hour last evening, had returned the verdict that the little girl 'came to her death at the hands of an unknown man in whose company said Goldie Williams was on the afternoon of Feb. 6, 1912.'"

The fervor to catch the cold-blooded murderer of the young girl from Grand Island quickly reached a crescendo, with everyone shouting for the killer's head.

On the same day the two arrests were reported, the *Sheboygan Journal* in Sheboygan, Wisconsin, echoed everyone's frustration when its headlines shouted, slayer of girl not found, followed by an account of the startling number of men hunting for the madman.

"Ten thousand men are searching a territory 100 miles square for the murderer of little Goldie Williams, whose body was found in a vacant house in Grand Island," the *Journal* stated about the crime now capturing national headlines. "The manhunt covers the entire central portion of Nebraska and is participated in practically by every man for 60 miles on all sides of this city. Dozens of posses of determined men are running races to see which will first discover and hang the murderer."

Newspapers from as far away as Benton Harbor, Michigan, and Carbondale, Illinois, tracked the progress in the hunt for the child's killer, telling readers that law enforcement officers were pursuing every lead, and traveling across the state to interrogate suspects picked up in other locations. Overall, the reports were not promising.

"Developments in the search for the murderer of Goldie Williams leave the authorities with few promising clues," *The Daily Free Press* in Carbondale reported. "Several lines have been followed to a conclusion, only to find the suspected man was not the one wanted. Various reports of arrests and rumors of lynching reached the authorities and newspaper, but were found later to be without foundation."

Days turned into weeks, with still no sign of the killer. Reluctantly, Grand Island residents returned to their jobs, and their farms, empty-handed.

A month after Goldie Williams was murdered and weeks after her funeral, the public learned of the lengths to which authorities had gone to locate her killer. On March 13, 1912, *The Evening Gazette* of Cedar Rapids, Iowa, told readers of an odd occurrence that took place during the search, which was now resulting in a lawsuit.

Under the headline STRANGE COINCIDENCE CAUSES DAMAGE ACTION, the *Gazette* informed readers of the lawsuit filed in Council Bluffs, Iowa, stating:

> A remarkable set of coincidences are brought to light in a damage suit just filed here against the Western Union Telegraph company by E. F. Bailey of this city. The action grows out of the atrocious murder of Goldie Williams at Grand Island, Neb., a few weeks ago.
>
> Mr. Bailey is a stepson of J. F. Williams, an official of the Union Pacific railroad company, who resides at Grand Island. Mr. Williams has a daughter named Goldie Williams and her age is just that of the girl of the same name who was murdered.
>
> When the newspapers here announced the murder of Goldie Williams, Mr. Bailey sent a telegram to his stepfather asking if it was true that his little half sister, Goldie, had been murdered. In the excitement occasioned by the terrible crime, when everything in the shape of clues were being sought and followed by the officers, the sheriff of Hall County, Neb., learned of the telegram from Council Bluffs and either had it delivered to him or at least got possession of it, and he then wired the Council Bluffs police officers to arrest Bailey.
>
> Acting upon these instructions, the police here placed Bailey under surveillance, but did not arrest him,

and it was three days before the fact was established that Mr. Bailey's stepfather is an entirely different person and in no way related to the father of the murdered girl. The telegram was then turned over to Mr. Williams.

Mr. Bailey claims to have been annoyed and humiliated and demands $3,000 of the telegraph company, $2,000 for failure to deliver the message promptly, and $1,000 for pain and humiliation.

More than a year later, on October 23, 1913, the case went to court, appropriately in the town of Correctionville, Iowa. Presumably, it was settled out of court by Western Union, as it was not mentioned in the newspaper again.

As spring gave way to summer in 1912, Grand Island farmers planted their sugar beets, tended their stock, and certainly lamented the circumstances that had allowed the killer of little Goldie Williams to go free.

That fall, Nebraskans and the rest of the nation went to the polls to elect a new president. Pitting Democrat Woodrow Wilson against incumbent Republican William Taft, the race was decidedly influenced by the third-party entry of former president, Theodore Roosevelt, making his bid on the "Bull Moose" ticket. In results echoed across the United States, T. R. captured 29 percent of Nebraska's votes to Taft's 21 percent, giving Wilson a landside victory with nearly 44 percent of the tally.

Two years after Goldie's untimely death, the "War to End All Wars" began in Europe, and soon U.S. forces were brought into the fray. For many Nebraskans, the horrific murder of the ten-year-old schoolgirl faded from view—except for one Grand Island resident, who would never forget what had happened to Goldie, and the man who had escaped any consequences for her murder.

William L. Cunningham had been a sixteen-year-old schoolboy when the body of little Goldie Williams had been discovered, sending the populace of the Grand Island area into a frenzy. And, like all men within 100 miles of the murder site, he had taken part in the unsuccessful search for her killer. Cunningham never forgot Goldie and her tragic end.

As a forty-one-year-old trying to eke out a living in the depths of the Great Depression, Cunningham moved to Colorado Springs, Colorado, in the summer of 1937. A painter by trade, he hoped to find more work on the growing Front Range of Colorado than he had found nearly 500 miles east in Nebraska. Little did he know, he was destined to find much more than work.

On a warm June night, Cunningham was exploring his new home of Colorado Springs, 70 miles south of Denver. As he walked through the downtown, a vivid boyhood recollection "of a man all the kids were afraid of" surged forward in his consciousness, as he stared at a gray-haired laborer stumbling down the street. A quarter-century had passed since he had last seen Charles Wesley Cox in Grand Island, the man who had disappeared at the same time Goldie Williams had. And now, through sheer happenstance, Cunningham had come across the man suspected of killing Goldie. Cunningham immediately went to the police and told them about his sighting of the now-sixty-one-year-old suspect. Police quickly located the five-foot-six, 142-pound rapist and murderer and took him into custody on the evening of June 24, 1937. Under intense questioning, Cox sang a long and sad song to the local district attorney.

Working as a janitor in Colorado Springs for the previous twelve years, Cox admitted that he was, indeed, the man who

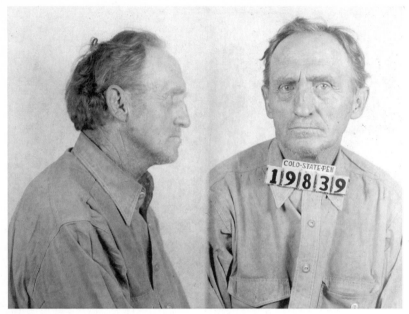

The 1937 prison mugshot of Charles Wesley Cox, taken by the Colorado Department of Corrections following the sentencing of Cox to fifty years to life for the rape of two young Fort Collins, Colorado, girls. Although he was never tried for the crime, Cox confessed to killing ten-year-old Goldie Williams in Grand Island, Nebraska, in 1912. *Photo courtesy of the Colorado State Archives*

had murdered the ten-year-old schoolgirl in Grand Island so many years before. District Attorney Clyde L. Starrett soon learned that Cox's penchant for small girls had never quite been requited.

The day after Cunningham's keen observation had led to Cox's arrest, newspapers across the U.S. touted the suspect's apprehension and his written confession in a news bulletin bearing a Colorado Springs dateline. "A 61-year-old man who 'displayed no remorse,' was held here today for the slaying 25 years ago of a 10-year-old Grand Island, Neb., girl, District Attorney Clyde L. Starrett said, and for the raping of two small Colorado Springs girls," the Associated Press reported. "Starrett announced he was preparing charges against Charles Wesley Cox based on the recent assault of the two girls, ages 7 and 9 years."

Authorities learned that the blue-eyed, ruddy-faced Cox was originally from Kansas, where his sister, Sharon, and brother, George, still lived; that he had been married and divorced, and enjoyed cigarettes and alcohol in liberal quantities; and that he could read and write, was a Methodist, and had never previously been incarcerated. He would now get that opportunity.

Through extended interviews with authorities, Cox revealed everything about the Grand Island murder and the more-recent Colorado Springs child rapes. Thinking back twenty-five years, he told the district attorney details of Goldie Williams's murder that only the killer could know: how he had lured the girl to the vacant house, raped and strangled her, beat her on the head with a hammer, secreted her limp body in the mortar box, and covered it with a door.

Armed with a signed confession, District Attorney Starrett completed his interrogation, prepared his charges, garnered a "guilty" plea from Cox, and only five days after Cox's arrest, got the murderer and rapist sentenced to fifty years to life in prison.

Shortly after his sentencing for rape on June 29, 1937, before an El Paso County, Colorado, judge, Cox was whisked away under heavy security to the Colorado State Penitentiary in Canyon City, Colorado, to begin serving his extended sentence as Inmate No. 19839.

It would not be a long stint. Just 891 days after he was confined, on December 7, 1939, Charles Wesley Cox died in the prison hospital of unrecorded causes.

Cox, the Nebraska outlaw who had committed heinous acts of depravity with young girls, killed at least one, evaded posses totaling 10,000 men, and remained on the lam for a quarter-century after the murder of Goldie Williams, was never tried for his crimes in the Cornhusker State.

Frank "The Omaha Sniper" Carter

Thought at varying times to be manic, tormented, or a drug-crazed addict, Frank Carter was, in fact, simply a dull man who sought the spotlight. None too intelligent as a young man, he seemed to only get dumber as he aged. Like table wine with a bad cork, by the time he reached midlife, he had arguably fermented into Nebraska's first mass murderer and one of its most notorious outlaws.

Born by some accounts in 1881 in County Mayo, Ireland, where he was named Patrick Murphy, he likely found his way to America on the trailing tide of several million Irish immigrants who had been stampeding across the Atlantic Ocean for the preceding three decades. Although he would later claim Kansas City, Missouri, as his home, evidence indicates that he was actually born in Ackley, Iowa, with the given name of Frank Louis Clark. Regardless of his origins, Carter didn't stay in one place long enough to establish any permanency.

In a lifetime of quiet crime, Carter would one day boast that he had committed more than fifty holdups in more than a dozen cities that included Chicago, Sioux City, Des Moines, Lincoln, St. Joseph, Missouri, and Kansas City, and that his name would be remembered long after Charles Lindbergh's was forgotten.

Nearing his thirty-fifth year of life, Carter found himself working as a laborer on a large farm near Orange City, smack dab in the middle of corn country in north-central Iowa. A common farmhand with no real experience or ambition, Carter had an innate desire to strive for success. As he approached middle age with no rainbow in sight, he found himself increasingly longing for power and fame. Despite his worst efforts, he would eventually find his power in the sights of a silenced weapon pointed at some hapless victim, trigger finger at the ready. As for fame—Carter was destined to have it follow him all the way to Nebraska's electric chair.

Stuck on the massive Iowa farm of a millionaire cowman in 1915, Frank Carter probably hated his very existence. As he performed his chores in winter, Carter struggled with ice, snow, and occasional blizzards that roared in from the northwest. In summer, he sweltered in this land of almost too much sky, far too much manual work, and all manner of insects.

Surrounded on a daily basis by his rich boss's impressive farmstead, including a spacious house, generous outbuildings, and the latest in gadgets—none of which he could claim for himself—resentment slowly built, until one day in 1916, Carter snapped. Grabbing his favorite .22 caliber rifle and a box of shells, he went hunting for domestic livestock. Unfortunately, the cows and horses he shot belonged to his employer, and the farmer was even less impressed than the livestock Carter left bleeding on the ground.

Quickly apprehended and jailed, Carter was soon tried and convicted for the crime. The judge sentenced the Irish immigrant turned cattle killer to four years in the Iowa state penitentiary at Fort Madison. While serving his extended stint in the pen, located on the Iowa-Illinois border, Carter focused on improving his skills. He became an expert electrician, and by the time he was released in 1920, friends had already secured him employment at the Swift Packing Co. in Sioux City, Iowa.

Although Carter flew under the radar of local law enforcement, evidence exists that he was not always law-abiding. Small holdups and petty larcenies committed in and around Sioux City would later be attributed to Carter.

But these crimes didn't hold a candle to what happened on a September day in 1924, when he walked into a Sioux City hardware store and left two bodies on the floor as he departed. The murders of William Lougherson and Harry Jones that fall day would remain unsolved for the next three years.

No one would ever truly know what set Carter off on his killing spree several months later, in February of 1926. Residents of Omaha soon realized that the body count was mounting, and local newspapers were recommending that home and business owners "black out" all their lights to prevent them from becoming a target for a gunman who was randomly selecting his victims. In a matter of days, businesses in Nebraska's largest city came to a standstill, streets emptied, and the bars, honky-tonks, and other entertainment venues of Omaha were cleared of customers for more than a week. The city was in a state of panic brought about by a lone gunman who was variously described as the "Maniac," the "Phantom Sniper," and the "Omaha Sniper."

On February 18, 1926, newspapers as far away as the *Tribune* in Oakland, California, carried a story bearing an Omaha dateline, under the headline MANIAC GUNMAN MURDERS DOCTOR. The brief report noted, "Police said this morning that a maniac who had spread terror in an Omaha neighborhood bordering the downtown district shot and killed Dr. A. D. Searles, Omaha specialist, last night. Dr. Searles was found shot to death in his office this morning. Several persons in Omaha have been hit by mysterious bullet(s). Dr. Searles is the second victim to be struck fatally."

The next day, the *Waterloo Evening Courier* announced on its front page that spent shell casings were the only clue to Omaha's death-dealing rifleman. The headline read: POLICE UP IN THE AIR, RESIDENTS TERROR-STRICKEN, AT MERCY OF KILLER, adding, "Two More Shot At; One Man Falls Dead," then adding again in subheads stacked four high, "Bullets Whiz By Sailor and Janitor in Night Filled with Fears." It got the public's attention, and it sold a lot of newspapers.

The day after the shootings, the *Courier* reported: "A handful of little copper rifle shells, left by the 'phantom rifleman' who has killed two persons with his silenced weapon and sent leaden pellets whirring too close to others for comfort, comprised the clues on which a frantic police force was working today."

The first shooting had occurred on Sunday night, when William McDevitt was hit four times (others say six) and killed while walking through an Omaha neighborhood. On Tuesday evening, the phantom sniper fired a round at a drugstore window in downtown Omaha. A spent shell casing was found across the street.

On Thursday night, more gunshots were scattered throughout Omaha. Dr. Searles, a prominent local physician, was killed in his office, though no one save the killer would know of that until Friday morning when, wondering what had kept him, his wife peeked through the mail slot of the doctor's door and discovered the grisly scene. Two other men were shot at during the night, and another died of heart trouble while discussing the activities of the "maniac sniper" who was haunting Omaha, the newspaper reporting that "Frank Pesek, 45, toppled over dead during an argument over the supposed madman."

The *Waterloo Evening Courier* reported:

> A shot in the dark that whistled uncomfortably close past his head was John Fitzhenry's introduction to Omaha. Fitzhenry, Detroit, Mich., sailor, and former Canadian soldier, had just arrived from San Diego, Cal., where he had been discharged from a Liverpool boat. He was walking a block from the main business district when he heard the shot and felt the bullet whiz by. He knew nothing of the activities of the maniac.

The AP reported that "John Turner, Negro janitor at a downtown office building, heard the shot and rushed outdoors. A bullet flattened itself against the building six inches above his head." The *Waterloo Evening Courier* continued: "Police confessed they were totally without clues and at a loss as to how to proceed in running down the slayer . . . Police of Omaha are confronted with a baffling series of shootings, believed to have been committed by a maniac or drug-crazed addict. Efforts to trap the mysterious assailant have proven fruitless, despite the stationing of numerous officers in the vicinity. The man will be caught—such persons always are—but the police are concerned lest he add others to his list of terrorism before they grab him."

As the manhunt intensified, so did the rising concerns of local residents, until the "excitement throughout Omaha . . . reached white heat," the Associated Press proclaimed. Newspapers posted $750 in rewards for the capture of the perpetrator, and the police department stepped up its efforts to corral the culprit, relying on .22 shell casings left at the scene of both killings, and the drugstore vandalism. "The city's nervousness was attested by scores of telephone calls for police aid, the reports ranging from actual shootings to flapping shutters. No trace of the rifleman was found, however."

As Omaha residents hunkered down, Carter roamed the streets as he pleased, proud of his actions and unafraid of being apprehended. The same day the Omaha sniper's story appeared in newspapers across the country, New York City developed its own "mad sniper." Four victims were shot down in the streets of the city's East Side, and "Happy Jimmy" Barnstory, a thirty-five-year-old black minstrel, was killed in the melee. No one saw the assailant, and police attributed the crimes to a trigger-happy copycat who had read of Carter's misdeeds.

Eventually, Carter headed south out of Omaha to Council Bluffs, where he had an unfortunate encounter with a railroad detective who was among scores of law enforcement officers ordered to be on the lookout for anyone suspicious. When detective Ross Johnston apparently took too keen an interest in the former farmhand, Carter shot him five times and left him to die. Before Johnston succumbed to his wounds, he gave police a description of his assailant.

Just as the situation reached a fever pitch in Omaha two weeks after the initial shootings, police in nearby Bartlett, Iowa, 31 miles south of Omaha, received a break in the case. They found Carter. Surrounded by well-armed lawmen, the suspect didn't even put up a fight or draw his treasured handgun, complete with a silencer. He simply smiled, raised his hands, waived extradition, and resigned himself to the media spotlight that awaited him.

Frank "The Omaha Sniper" Carter, in handcuffs, following his capture by authorities in Bartlett, Iowa. *Photo courtesy of the* Omaha World-Herald

While in custody, Carter told authorities that he wanted to pay the penalty for his crimes as quickly as possible, adding that he preferred to be hanged. "But if it's the chair, I'll walk to it like a man," he said. Transported back to Omaha, authorities said they would give Carter "the speediest trial ever staged," swift justice for the man who had so frightened their community.

"Efforts will be made to try and sentence to death within ten days the man who terrorized Omaha for a week, County Attorney (Henry) Beal announced." The real identity of the suspect—Louis Clark—was revealed after he was recognized by a state agent who knew him during his Iowa penitentiary days. Delighted with Carter's capture, the town breathed a collective sigh of relief, and the word soon spread across the nation.

PHANTOM SNIPER NOW IN CUSTODY, screamed the February 23 front page of the *Indiana Evening Gazette*. Beneath the banner, a subhead announced, "Frank Carter, 46, Confesses to Multitude of Crimes."

The article went on to say a Dr. F. S. Lovely had conducted a complete medical exam of the suspect and found that he was suffering from paresis, the last stages of a loathsome social disease. After the examination, the *Waterloo Evening Gazette* claimed that Carter was so sick he would never see the electric chair. "Carter will be dead or a raving maniac before the legal machinery putting him to death can be operated, the doctors say."

Police also took the opportunity to tell reporters that they believed Carter was the man responsible for the September 1924 murders of William Lougherson and Harry Jones in a Sioux City hardware store. While he denied committing the killings, Carter did tell police that he had carried a .22 caliber automatic for two years since purchasing it through a mail-order house, and that he had staged more than fifty holdups from Chicago to Lincoln to Kansas City.

"I always had trouble making my victims respect my small-caliber gun," Carter said. "When they laugh at it they make me mad and I shoot them." Remarking on Carter's interview, reporters wrote, "Carter is proud of his crime record. He tells the story with a great deal of bravado and a wealth of detail. He killed both Dr. A. D. Searles and William McDevitt because they failed to 'show proper respect for his small pistol.'"

In the aftermath of the gunman's apprehension, authorities released a lengthy statement gleaned from extended interviews with Carter.

"In a statement covering more than a score of pages, the man held for the deaths of two men, the serious wounding of a third, the frightening of a girl when he shot through a window into a drugstore, and the terrorizing of two cities for many nights, detailed his shootings and motives, according to Henry Beal, county attorney," one newspaper reported. "The killing of Dr. A. D. Searles, according to the statement, was because the physician would not give him money; William L. McDevitt, dairyman, was shot to death on the street two weeks ago because Carter, his statement said, feared McDevitt was after him; the same reason was given for the shooting in Council Bluffs of Ross Johnston, Railroad detective."

Carter would later be implicated in a number of crimes, including the murder of an Iowa trapper, Ed Riley. Investigators revealed that the unfortunate trapper had been shot in the head with a .22 caliber bullet, and then his body had been staked to the bottom of the Little Sioux River.

Though justice was indeed speedy by today's standards, it took some time to bring the "Phantom Sniper" to trial, and for his attorneys to exhaust his seemingly endless appeals. At his month-long trial, Carter's attorneys argued for an insanity defense, but the jury quickly convicted him of the murders of Dr. Searles and McDevitt, and even more expeditiously, the judge sentenced Carter to die in Nebraska's electric chair.

Before his scheduled date of execution, Carter spoke freely with investigators regarding his assorted crimes, and with reporters eager to discern where the middle-aged man had gone wrong. Frank Carter, alias Louis Clark, told newsmen he had killed forty-three people in his life, and that the list included the unsolved Villisca, Iowa, ax murders, committed fifteen years earlier, when an entire family was wiped out. While authorities discounted that claim, they told reporters they did believe Carter's confession that he had murdered a hardware merchant and his son in Sioux City in 1925.

On June 23, 1927, the Nebraska Supreme Court refused to grant a stay of Carter's planned execution. Before the sun rose the next morning, Frank Carter was awake in his jail cell, awaiting his breakfast and his final day on earth. His last meal consisted of bacon and eggs, and he told assembled reporters that he had slept very well, and that he was "ready to have it over with."

He accompanied his jailers to the death chamber unassisted, and glanced unconcernedly at the group of officials and newspapermen gathered to watch his execution. With no outward signs of emotion, the Omaha sniper helped his guards and the executioner as they strapped him into the chair in which he would die.

As the executioner was adjusting the "death mask" on Carter's head, the condemned man protested that it was not necessary as far as he was concerned. After the hood was fastened, the doomed man whispered, "Turn on the juice." Six minutes after being placed in the chair, Frank Carter, one of Nebraska's most unusual outlaws, was pronounced dead.

Grandma Terror—Annie Cook

Steeped in the Prohibition years of the 1920s, the story of Annie Cook is one of a venomous Nebraska outlaw who never had enough, and didn't hesitate to cajole, belittle, bribe, beat, or exterminate anyone who stood in her way. Indeed, slender little Annie Cook's true story is more terrifying than the legends and lore of any of the Cornhusker State's many cattle rustlers, bank bandits, train robbers, and gunmen.

Annie Cook was born on July 15, 1873, in Denver, Colorado, the daughter of moderately wealthy Jewish parents who had emigrated from Russia and opened a thriving livery stable in the fledgling community. Every member of the large family worked hard to get ahead, even Annie and her sister, Lizzie. Annie didn't mind the day-to-day drudgery of life on the Western frontier, but as a young woman, she did experience a growing resentment over the fact that she didn't get paid for her honest labor, while the men in the family, including her brothers, did.

When a tall, handsome young farmer from Nebraska, Frank Cook, stopped at the livery stable for supplies one day in 1893, nineteen-year-old Annie saw an opportunity that could help define her future, while removing her from the unappreciated labors of her family's business. She befriended the likable man, who owned a farmstead near Hershey, Nebraska.

By all accounts, Frank was an earnest, well-liked young farmer content to work his small 80-acre spread and enjoy his neighbors. He didn't necessarily want to own the largest farm in Lincoln County; Frank just wanted to live a life free of major stress and worry. When he took Annie as his wife, the odds of that tranquil existence actually coming to pass vanished like topsoil in a tornado.

You see, Annie wanted it all—money, land, and power. And for the next few decades, she would expend all of her nastiness to pursue her own dreams, even if they were contrary to her husband's. Once she arrived on his diminutive farm outside Hershey in the winter of 1893, Annie assessed her husband's operation and found it wanting in virtually every respect. The house was too small, there was an insufficient amount of tillable land, and, without acquiring additional property, there would be no prospect of living the kind of life she had planned for herself.

In this regard, Annie wasn't alone. In the last part of the nineteenth century, many Americans were transfixed by the possibility of creating something from nothing, of living a life of luxury in which their well-considered schemes and lucrative deals could replace the hard work and endless toil on which the nation had been built. From Wall Street to Main Street, promoters and confidence men were striking it rich by wheeling and dealing their way to wealth.

The same year Annie was born in Denver, Mark Twain and Charles Dudley Warner penned *The Gilded Age*, presenting a satirical account of political corruption and financial greed in post–Civil War America. The book's central character, Colonel Beriah Sellers, was a honey-tongued promoter whose eloquence served as "a magician's wand that turned dried apples into figs and water into wine as easily as it could turn a hovel into a palace and present poverty into future riches."

Armed with that notion that she, too, could create something from the nothing that was her husband's farm, Annie set about exploiting everyone around her. Frank was constantly belittled, and when a daughter, Clara, was born three years after they wed, she was engaged in involuntary servitude essentially from the time she could walk.

When things became too bleak on the isolated farm in 1905, Annie boarded a train to travel east to Nebraska's largest town of Omaha, ostensibly to see a doctor for a recurring bladder infection. The doctor quickly diagnosed the problem, prescribed medication, and told her to return to see him in a week. While in the waiting room, Annie met the madam of a local "sporting house," who would spend the next week moving Annie from a low-end hotel to her own establishment, buying her fashionable clothes, educating Annie on the application of rouge, eye shadow, mascara, and lipstick, and the proper etiquette of entertaining moneyed men.

As her one-week stay stretched into a month, Annie found herself with a suitcase of stylish clothes she could never wear in Hershey, and more money than she had ever had in her life. She reluctantly returned to the drab surroundings of the farm with a renewed purpose, and the realization that she now had the means to execute her plan. She told Frank that the doctor had diagnosed a chronic condition that would require her periodic return to Omaha, and thus the stage was set for the thirty-one-year-old farm wife. For the next two decades, Annie's occasional work as a prostitute would provide the continuing income with which to fund her fondest desires.

Neglecting her young daughter, Annie set about improving the farm, and nearly drove her husband to exhaustion in the process.

They raised poultry, sold eggs and holiday turkeys, planted corn and potato crops, tended apple and cherry trees, milked cows and churned butter. Following the harvest of 1898, with the help of Annie's supplemental income, the couple paid off the mortgage and Annie set her sights on buying the neighboring farm.

That same fall, Annie's parents came to visit from Denver with her sister, Lizzie. By the time their parents departed, Annie had agreed to let Lizzie stay on the farm. The arrangement was enticing to Annie because first, her sister could be another free hand for the farm, and, second, their parents planned to leave their large Denver home and a portion of their estate to Lizzie. Annie had little doubt that Lizzie's inheritance would one day be her very own.

Before their parents' train had even left the station, Annie was barking orders to her shy sister, telling her that she must pay her way by milking the cows, churning the butter, collecting eggs, planting and harvesting, and dressing poultry. In addition, Lizzie must make little four-year-old Clara into a productive member of the family. Intimidated by her older sister, Lizzie quickly agreed.

Unknown to Annie, Lizzie had developed a relationship with a rancher named Joe Knox from the Nebraska Sandhills. The two kept up a clandestine relationship through the mail. One day, when Frank, Annie, and Clara were in town delivering cream, butter, and eggs, Knox came to call on Liz. When he presented her with a Christmas present, Lizzie broke down and wept, confessing that she had never worked so hard in her life, providing details of her domineering sister. Knox promised to return in the spring to marry her and take her back to the Sandhills, where she would never have to work that hard again.

When Knox wrote to Lizzie again in the spring, he said he would be in North Platte on the night of May 28, 1901, and that she should meet him at the courthouse the next morning for their marriage ceremony. And that's exactly what Lizzie did. While Annie was busy in the farmhouse kitchen, Lizzie stole away down the country lane toward town, eventually catching a ride to the courthouse with a soft-hearted farmer headed in the same direction. Finding Knox waiting in front of the courthouse, the two quickly bought their license to wed, walked down the hall to the office of the Justice of the Peace, and were married. The couple then climbed into Knox's wagon and traveled two days to the Sandhills and their new home together.

Meanwhile, Annie was despondent over Lizzie's defection. She had lost a valuable farm worker and was likely to lose Liz's inheritance as well. When Annie learned where Lizzie had gone, she traveled to the Sandhills, but couldn't convince her sister to return to the farm. She also journeyed to Denver, lied to her parents about her sister's absence, and found out everything she could about Joe Knox. Later that year, when their mother died, Annie returned to Denver for the funeral, making excuses for Lizzie's absence. When their father decided to move in with one of his sons, Annie quickly put the big house, bequeathed to her sister, up for sale and returned to Hershey.

Angered that she now had to tend to the farm chores previously performed by Lizzie, Annie worked hard on the farm and plotted her revenge. In July 1902, Lizzie gave birth to a daughter, and she and Joe Knox named her Mary. As the months turned into years, Annie bided her time and schemed to get her sister back into her fold. In the spring of 1905, Annie wrote Lizzie a well-crafted letter, inviting her and her daughter to come back to Hershey for a visit, promising that she wouldn't have to work, and that Annie would buy her beloved little sister some new clothes. Unfortunately, Lizzie took the bait.

When she arrived in Hershey that spring with her daughter in tow, Lizzie quickly realized that nothing had changed with Annie. Her gruff sister ordered her to milk the cows that very night, and the next day Lizzie was forced to clean the chicken coops and the cow barns, and care for the poultry. Secretly, because Annie wouldn't even let her go near the mailbox, Lizzie sent her husband a card that implored him, "Don't write, just come."

In a matter of days, Joe Knox showed up at the Cook farm and demanded that his family be allowed to leave with him. Annie's answer was decidedly succinct: She grabbed her shotgun, pointed it at Joe's chest, and demanded that he get off her property. Unarmed, Knox relented, promising his wife that he would return. A few days later, over Lizzie's objections, Annie sent little Mary off to live with their brother in Colorado. Joe did return several times, and was run off at gunpoint. When he came with a lawyer, Annie only laughed and pointed her shotgun at the pair. Joe Knox would never return.

Bolstered by her sinister success, Annie put Frank, Lizzie, and Clara to work every morning at 4:00 a.m. When Lizzie's daughter, Mary, turned five, Annie traveled to her brother's residence in Denver, told them that Lizzie was very sick, and that she needed to take Mary back to Hershey to be with her mother. When they returned to the farm a few days later, Annie immediately put the five-year-old to work collecting eggs. Mary was punished for every one she broke. And one night, when an innocent little mole on Mary's right cheek caught Annie's attention, the villain put a poker in the stove, heated it to red hot, and then burned it off her niece's face.

As Prohibition came to the land in the 1920s, North Platte—just 15 miles from Hershey—became known as "Little Chicago." City officials turned a blind eye to the gambling, illegal alcohol, prostitution, and extortion in their town in exchange for copious quantities of hush money. Annie Cook wasn't above paying bribes to any of them.

When her daughter Clara reached the eighth grade, Annie wondered how she might best be put to use in her grand plan. Annie decided to enroll her in the high school in North Platte, and purchased a home where she and Clara could live while they were in town. It all looked innocent enough, until Annie took on a "boarder"—an attractive young woman who would live at the house and watch Clara when Annie had to be out at the farm. In fact, Annie had hired the woman away from the best bordello in town. By the end of the school year, Annie had four "boarders" living at the house, and she was able to purchase a beautiful new two-seater carriage with a fringed canopy top.

Back at the farm, Annie remained a wicked taskmaster, barking orders and beating little Mary with a buggy whip until her legs bled.

When Clara turned thirteen, her mother decided it was time for a coming out, although it didn't involve a party. Annie and Clara boarded a train for Omaha, where Annie's old friend, the sporting-house madam, introduced the teenager to the rewards of prostitution. Two years later, when Clara turned fifteen, Annie entered into negotiations with an older North Platte businessman of Japanese descent, who was infatuated with Clara. At the conclusion of the talks, Annie had agreed to sell her daughter to the man for the princely sum of $500. There were conditions: The gentleman was not to visit Clara more than three times a week, and she would have to finish high school.

The next year, when a Union Pacific railroad crew set up camp near the Cook farm, Annie met with the supervisor and made an arrangement. For several weeks, she and her sixteen-year-old daughter serviced the crews, enriching their bank account by several hundred dollars. A year later, Annie established her second "house" in North Platte and hired an experienced madam to run it. By now, she was well on her way to wealth and creating the life she had always dreamed of for herself.

In her definitive biography of Annie Cook, titled *Evil Obsession*, author Nellie Snyder Yost tells of the dirt-poor itinerant farm workers hired by Annie to work their sugar beet fields in the summer of 1915. With a thunderstorm fast approaching, Annie was worried that the work wouldn't get done and that the rain would delay a return to the fields for several days. As she approached a pregnant Hispanic woman whose family had been hired to work the fields, cracking her whip and yelling at everyone to work faster, the pregnant woman stood up and gripped her sides.

" 'Missus,' the woman gasped, her face twisting in pain as she tried to tell Annie, with her few English words, that she needed to go back to the shack, her baby was coming.

" 'No,' Annie shouted. 'You're not stopping work. You lazy bitches sluff [sic] off on the job every chance you get, but you damn well won't get away with it in my fields. Get to choppin', damn you,' and she swung the whip at the woman. With a look of despair, she bent to her task again."

Half an hour later, the Mexican woman simply fell to the ground and, in a matter of minutes, gave birth to twin sons right there in the furrows of the sugar beet field. Ordering young Mary to cart the newborns to the itinerant family's shack, Annie then berated and whipped the woman who had just delivered the babies until, reluctantly, she bent down and continued her field work.

With her mounting wealth, Annie continued implementing her grand plan in incremental steps. By 1923, she had greased enough palms of city and county officials—and threatened others with exposure for their sexual proclivities—to gain the contract for the Lincoln County Poor Farm, which forever after was known as Cook Poor Farm. While the patients had previously been treated with dignity and respect, Annie treated them with contempt and made them work on the farm as slave labor. Some ran away. Others who too strenuously objected to Annie's treatment mysteriously disappeared or were found floating facedown in the farm's irrigation ditches.

Meanwhile, Frank was despondent over the way Annie treated her sister Lizzie, and young Mary. But, in a contest of wills, he was powerless to fight Annie. Finally, when Annie accused her husband of sexually assaulting Clara, whom he loved, Frank moved his quarters into the barn, where he would stay until he died in 1936.

Bolstered by her success, Annie began dabbling in bootleg whiskey and buying tax-delinquent properties, bribing the local sheriff to evict the unfortunate tenants, then reselling them at a handsome profit. She built a gleaming new white farmhouse to replace the old one, which was now being used to house the indigents of Lincoln County. By 1920, she was driving around town in a sparkling new Ford touring car and hoarding all her cash at home.

For a dozen more years, Annie's life went on this way: badgering and bullying her family and the Poor Farm workers, and bribing city and county officials to look the other way over conditions at the Poor Farm, her houses of prostitution, her bootlegging, and her other nefarious activities. With regularity, she also argued with her daughter, Clara, who had gradually tired of her mother's meanness. They screamed and swore a blue streak, and didn't care who knew it.

On May 29, 1934, the constant bickering and battles came to a head. Clara screamed at her mother for the last time, then exited the house and stormed into the yard. Enraged, Annie followed her out the door with a heavy lid-lifter from the stove in her hand; without thought, she threw it at her retreating daughter. The lid-lifter struck Clara on the back of her head. Dazed by the blow, Clara ran around a tree in the yard two or three times, "like a chicken with its head cut off, and then just fell down dead."

The next day, the *Daily Bulletin* erroneously reported in a front-page headline, CLARA COOK DEAD, VICTIM OF POISON. The newspaper claimed in its story that the thirty-eight-year-old operator of the county Poor Farm died after an inmate of the Home allegedly prepared a dose of disinfectant for her, believing it was the medicine she had requested. Further, the county attorney, clerk, and commissioner had investigated the incident and did not believe an inquest was warranted, the *Daily Bulletin* reported.

Annie showed up at her daughter's funeral and grieved in a manner appropriate to the occasion. She soon lost the contract to maintain the county Poor Farm, which she and Clara had held for the previous twelve years. But her daughter's untimely death was not without its rewards. Shortly after the funeral, she met with insurance investigators and demanded that they pay double indemnity on the $10,000 insurance policy Annie had taken out on Clara, because she had died in an accidental manner. With the ill-gotten gains, Annie was able to purchase the 80 acres of farmland that she had coveted for nearly forty years, and buy a new car, which coincidentally she had denied her daughter when she was alive.

Annie Cook would live for another eighteen years after murdering her daughter in a fit of rage. Those who knew her say she didn't get any nicer, didn't play any fairer, and didn't really give a second thought to the manner in which she had lived her life. Only when Annie died on May 27, 1952, did her sister, Lizzie, escape from the clutches of the woman who was, perhaps, Nebraska's meanest and most feared outlaw.

The Ma Barker Gang

Even today, a casual visitor can see the bullet holes in the floor of the old bank in Fairbury, Nebraska, a lasting testament to a bloody day in 1932 when machine guns fired, windows shattered, people screamed, and seven fell to the ground in agony, hit in the cross fire.

The outlaw trail of Ma Barker and her boys is as vicious and violent as any in the American West, a blood-strewn track littered with kidnappings, killings, raids, and robberies. Partially credited with being the impetus for J. Edgar Hoover's "War on Crime," this formidable criminal clan, made up of the Barker boys, Alvin Karpis, Sam Taran, and other gun-wielding thugs, wreaked havoc in America's heartland, which ended in a Florida shoot-out that lasted for hours.

Ma Barker, the motherly matron immortalized as the gang's leader, and eventually gunned down by the FBI with a shotgun in her hands, likely just came along for the ride.

It's believed that Arizona "Arrie" Clark, as Ma Barker was originally known, was born in Ash Grove, Missouri, on October 8, 1873. Married at eighteen to George Barker, a wandering worker, the couple had four boys named Fred, Arthur, Lloyd, and Herman. None would amount to much. In fact, early in their careers of crime, they would be known as the "Bloody Barkers."

At one point in the late 1920s, the dirt-poor Barkers could tell their friends that their sons were currently incarcerated in the federal penitentiary at Leavenworth, Kansas, the Kansas

State Prison, and the Oklahoma State Prison, while the final son, Herman, had committed suicide during a shoot-out with police in Wichita.

It was while serving a stint in the Kansas State Penitentiary at Lansing for bank burglary that Fred Barker met petty criminal Alvin Karpis, a brash young bandit who had been jailed for burglary, escape, and auto theft. They would form a lifelong alliance, though in relative terms of the average life expectancy for machine-gun-toting bank robbers, the alliance really didn't last that long.

When Karpis was released from prison in the spring of 1931, smack dab in the middle of America's Dust Bowl and with half of the population out of work, it was natural that he'd return to his life of crime. Hooking up with Fred Barker in Tulsa, Oklahoma, the pair would enlist criminals, thieves, and other assorted deadbeats to form a criminal enterprise that would raise the hackles of every bank president, train engineer, and wealthy individual in the Midwest for the next four years.

The early 1930s suddenly became the age of public enemies, G-men, and outlaws whose colorful monikers—such as Baby Face Nelson, Bonnie and Clyde, Pretty-Boy Floyd, Machine-Gun Kelly, and John Dillinger—would command America's headlines and capture readers' attention at a time when they welcomed any escape. Perhaps none of these outlaw gangs would attract more attention from the federal government and the press than Ma Barker and her merry band of bandits.

Although Ma Barker certainly protected her boys and accompanied them on their excursions to faraway bank vaults and stately mansions, contemporary historians, aided by later biographies and interviews of the gang's members and associates, argue that the old woman was not the criminal captain the FBI contended at the time. In fact, one known associate of the Barker-Karpis gang wrote that Ma Barker "couldn't plan breakfast," let alone mastermind a bank heist. Others have stated that the Barker boys would drop their mother at a movie theater where she would watch the newsreels while they committed their crimes.

Regardless of the extent of Ma Barker's leadership, the gang quickly established itself as greedy, elusive, and deadly.

Committing a series of burglaries and robberies in Tulsa, then moving on to Arkansas and Missouri, the gang left behind the body of police chief Manley Jackson and sheriff C. Roy Kelly before 1931 came to a close. In April 1932, the body of another victim, A. W. Dunlap, was found near a Minnesota lake. Two months later, seven members of the gang stormed and robbed a bank in Fort Scott, Kansas. That led to the arrest and imprisonment of three of the gang's roster, but Fred Barker and Karpis remained on the run, recruiting new members along the way.

Five weeks later, they hit the Cloud County Bank in Concordia, Kansas. In mid-August, they attacked, shot, and killed Tulsa attorney J. Earl Smith at his country club, after Smith failed to win the release of one of their cronies who had been tried for the Fort Scott job. A month later, Arthur "Doc" Barker was released from prison and joined the gang.

On December 16, 1932, the Barker-Karpis gang mounted their most ambitious raid to date, sporting submachine guns as they robbed the Third Northwestern National Bank in downtown Minneapolis. In the wake of their liberal dispersal of bullets in the bank heist, they left behind the bodies of one civilian and two policemen.

Dead at the scene was veteran police officer Ira L. Evans. Wounded was policeman Leo R. Gorski, "who was shot in the neck with a sub-machine gun bullet," according to the United Press reports. Gorski would die the next day. "Evans and Gorski were mowed down by a withering blast of machine-gun fire as they drove up to the bank in a police radio car in answer to a burglar alarm which had been set off when the bandits entered the institution."

Fifteen minutes after the gunmen blasted their way out of the bank, a "flash" was delivered to the Minneapolis police headquarters that St. Paul police had the gang surrounded in Como Park and cruisers rushed to the scene.

Armed with $25,000 in cash from the Minneapolis heist, the gang raced to St. Paul, where they began transferring the stolen loot to a second getaway car. When passerby Oscar Erickson paid too close attention to their nefarious activities, they shot him in the head.

Four days later, police announced that they were holding Lawrence DeVolt, alias Lawrence Barker, on suspicion of first-degree murder of the cops. Authorities also were holding a dozen other men and women in jail, conducting interrogations, running them through police lineups, and trying to catch every outlaw connected to the "robber gang" that killed their fellow officers.

Meanwhile, flush with cash, the remaining members of the Barker-Karpis gang likely spent the rest of the winter in the sun and sand of one of their Florida hideouts. But, by spring, they were ready to mount their next offensive and replenish their coffers with more tainted money.

On the first Tuesday in April 1933, Fred and Doc Barker, joined by Karpis, Taran, and two of their cronies, found themselves in the Nebraska town of Fairbury. The small town, tucked in the southeast corner of the state, was located just a few miles west of Rock Creek Station, where Wild Bill Hickok had made his name in a gunfight with the McCanles brothers seventy-two years earlier.

Brazen and bold, the half-dozen heavily armed bandits arrived in downtown Fairbury in their big, black sedan just as businesses were opening their doors for the day. The outlaws set their sights on the First National Bank, located on the town's busiest trading corner. One of the gang manned his machine gun directly in front of the bank. Another watched the getaway car. The remaining four desperadoes strode into the financial institution just after clerks had unlocked the doors, and one mounted his machine gun in the bank lobby.

Commanded to "stretch out on the floor," the bank's sixteen employees, including its president, did as instructed. The robbers hit the just-filled cash drawers and the vault, filling bags with currency and ready to make a quick exit.

Simultaneously, just across the street from the bank in the local courthouse, Jefferson County deputy sheriff W. S. Davidson was meeting with Peter Johnson, a traveling salesman for a law officers' supply house. Alerted to a commotion in the street with screams from passersby, Davidson and Johnson rushed out of the courthouse to investigate. Armed with revolvers and confronted by gangsters toting machine guns and shielded by civilian hostages, it would prove to be an unfortunate day on which to play hero. Newspapers nationwide would tell the tale the following day.

According to United Press reports on April 4, 1933:

> Six machine-gun-armed bandits robbed the First
> National Bank of $27,613 today, abducted two women
> and shot their way to freedom. The women were later
> released. Keith Sexton, bank clerk, was shot five times
> when the bandits forced him to serve as a shield as they
> left the bank. He was reported near death.
>
> Jefferson County deputy sheriff W. S. Davidson and
> Pete Johnson, of Des Moines, Iowa, were wounded in
> the exchange of gunfire. One bandit was wounded in the
> shoulder as the raiders' big black automobile sped down
> the street.
>
> Miss Wilma Vaughn and Mrs. Francis Wilson, bank
> employees, were ordered into the bandit car and taken as
> hostages by the men. They were dumped from the car,
> unhurt, 3 miles northeast of here.
>
> Sixteen bank employees, including bank president
> Luther Bonham, were forced to lie on the floor while the
> bandits looted the safe.
>
> The $27,613 taken was in currency, bank officials
> said. A few government securities were also taken.

Meanwhile, an Associated Press story that hit the wires the
same day reported:

> Captained by a man bank employees described as a
> "veteran robber," the bandits rushed into the bank
> shortly after it opened, terrorized employees and
> customers with threats of opening fire with the machine
> gun in the bank lobby, dashed to their car with two bank
> employees and two women customers as shields from the
> guns of officers and escaped.
>
> With drawn guns, [Deputy Sheriff Davidson and
> Johnson] ran into the street and opened fire on the
> robbers. Davidson was wounded in the leg and Johnson
> in the shoulder. Keith Sexton, bank employee forced into
> the street by robbers as a shield, was wounded five times
> when he came into the line of fire of the sub-machine
> gun with which the robbers returned the officers fire. His
> condition is critical.

Employees of the First National Bank of Fairbury, Nebraska, pose the day after a daring daylight robbery by the Barker-Karpis Gang in April 1933. *Photo courtesy of First National Bank/Vern Pfaff and Tiffany Sherwood*

First National Bank employees in Fairbury, Nebraska, reenact the positions they took on April 4, 1933, when bandits armed with machine guns stormed the bank and robbed it of more than $150,000. *Photo courtesy of First National Bank/Vern Pfaff and Tiffany Sherwood*

Initial estimates released by bank officials and police placed the loss at nearly $28,000. However, that number would later be revised to show the Barker-Karpis gang had actually relieved the bank of assets valued at more than $150,000, big money in the Dirty Thirties. Newspapers across the country soon began comparing the daring desperadoes' tactics and penchant for firing guns to the fabled gunslingers of the Wild West a half-century earlier.

"A modernized version of a typical Jesse James raid was enacted Tuesday by six machine-gun bandits who looted the First National Bank here of $27,643 and engaged in a furious battle with officers that left seven wounded," The *Daily Mail* in Hagerstown, Maryland, reported the day after the heist. "Shattered windows of business establishments and shot-perforated buildings attested to the exchange of shots between the desperadoes and police.

"Two bank employees were slugged when they were tardy in obeying the desperadoes' command to 'stretch out on the floor.' All were recovering tonight."

Though the caper at Fairbury's bank would be their largest haul, it certainly didn't signify the end of the bandits' criminal activities in the state of Nebraska. Five days after shooting out the lights of Fairbury, the Associated Press reported on the Barker-Karpis gang's continued success in their romp across the Cornhusker State. On April 9, the *Billings Gazette* told its Montana readers:

> Nebraska's loss to bank robbers this week stood at approximately $163,000 Saturday, after the $10,400 obtained by two gunmen from the Central City National Bank was added. The last of the three holdups came

five minutes before closing time Friday at the Central
City bank. Practically all the loot was in currency, and
a perfunctory check showed no bonds missing. No one
was hurt. The robbers apparently escaped.

Tuesday six machine-gunners invaded the First
National Bank of Fairbury, gathered up approximately
$26,000 in cash and securities to bring the total loot to
$152,000, and shot their way to freedom. Seven were
wounded, including one escaped gunman.

Monday the Carroll State Bank was robbed of $150
in cash by three men. They also escaped. No one was
injured.

With a comfortable stash of cash, the gang elected to lie low
for the next month. They would use that time to plan bigger
and bolder jobs with higher potential payouts. But, on May 8,
gang member and tough Sam Taran was arrested in St. Paul in
connection with the Nebraska bank robberies.

"Sam Taran, former pugilist and now president of the Util-
ity Finance Co., was arrested today on a warrant charging bank
robbery issued by Fairbury, Neb., authorities," The *Brainerd
Daily Dispatch* told readers. "Police said that half a dozen victims of a holdup of The First National bank of Fairbury had
identified a picture of Taran as one of six machine-gun bandits
who robbed the bank of $152,000 in cash and bonds.

"The warrant was issued after the appearance in St. Paul of
$4,000 worth of bonds said to be part of the loot. Taran said he
would fight extradition."

And, he did. But, Taran also apparently alienated some of
his fugitive friends in the process. Eighteen months after his
initial arrest, someone tried to blow him up.

"An attempt on the life of Sam Taran, notorious St. Paul
police character, was made here today when a bomb exploded

outside his bedroom window," the AP said on December 13, 1934. "Taran was in Chicago and other members of the household escaped uninjured, although windows were shattered and a section of the foundation was blown out.

"Last February Taran was freed in Chicago on charges instituted in Fairbury, Neb., following a $152,000 bank robbery there. Bonds stolen in the holdup appeared in St. Paul. When other loot from the robbery showed up in Chicago, it was allegedly traced to Taran, who was charged with receiving stolen property."

It would take district attorneys and the courts another eighteen months to put Taran away in prison, where he remained unappreciated.

While Taran was paying defense attorneys and doing his best to avoid extended prison time, other members of the Barker-Karpis gang were out working their way through the criminal world.

In June 1933, just two months after the Fairbury robbery, William Hamm, the young heir to the wealthy Hamm's Brewery dynasty, was kidnapped in the Twin Cities and held for ransom. The prominent family from the "Land of Sky Blue Waters," as their beer ads proclaimed, ponied up $100,000 and Hamm was released on June 19.

Six weeks later, the bandit boys hit the payroll of the Stockyards National Bank in South St. Paul, and, in a practice that was beginning to look like a sick habit, they executed policeman Leo Pavlak and crippled a second officer. Three weeks later, in mid-September, the gangsters held up two bank messengers and murdered another policeman who just happened to be investigating a nearby traffic accident.

As successful as 1933 had been for the Barker-Karpis gang, they set their sights on making their biggest score early in the new year.

On January 17, 1934, they snatched St. Paul banker Edward George Bremer, whose wealthy father was the majority owner of the Jacob Schmidt Brewing Co., and a personal friend of President Franklin Roosevelt. Following the Hamm abduction, Bremer had employed a bodyguard for a time, but had released him several weeks before his own kidnapping.

The abduction would prove quite lucrative, but in the wake of the kidnapping and killing of Charles Lindbergh's baby and a public outcry over abductions for ransom, this major crime would bring the full attention of the federal government to bear on this criminal syndicate, and would eventually spell the demise of the Barker-Karpis gang.

For more than two weeks, the outlaws held Bremer, president and owner of the Commercial State Bank, in a remote location, planning ransom demands and going over the intricacies of the exchange of their captive for a mountain of cash. On February 7, 1934, their demands were met, and near-breathless newspaper reports touted the massive amount of the ransom that had been paid.

The seventy-three-year-old Bremer also told the press of the personal note to the kidnappers that he included with the $200,000 in ransom money, not knowing if his son would truly be released if he made the payoff.

"To parties holding Edward," the note read. "I've done my part and kept my word 100 per cent just as I said I would. This money is not marked and is the full amount asked for. And now boys, I am counting on your honor. Be sports and do the square thing by turning Edward loose at once. Adolf Bremer."

The extended article went on to describe the tearful reunion of the thirty-seven-year-old Edward Bremer with his wife and daughter, and the activities of federal agents in hunting down the kidnappers.

"The attractive wife of the young banker hastened from her husband's home to that of the father-in-law. There was a joyful reunion as she hugged her husband. Bremer swept his daughter, Betty, aged 9, into his arms," the newspaper reported.

The exploits of the Barker-Karpis gang would grow to include train and mail robberies, extortion, protection from police officials paid off with ill-gotten gains, the outright purchase of paroles for their allies in crime, and even the armed robbery of police stations, where the gang would make late-night stops to acquire more machine guns.

With more money than they could count from the successful kidnappings, the gang wove their way through 1934 in style, while their contemporaries, such as John Dillinger, Pretty Boy Floyd, Baby Face Nelson, and Bonnie and Clyde, were all killed in shoot-outs with the FBI and other law enforcement agencies.

But, 1935 would prove to be a year of atonement for gang members. On the night of January 8, Doc Barker and his moll left his posh Chicago residence near Lake Michigan, only to be apprehended by FBI agents. When Chicago FBI chief Melvin Purvis asked Doc where his gun was, the legendary outlaw purportedly responded, "Home, and ain't that a helluva place for it?"

In a matter of months, Doc was put on trial for the Bremer kidnapping, convicted, and sentenced to serve the rest of his life at the federal prison located on Alcatraz Island. Among his fellow inmates would be George "Machine Gun" Kelly, Al Capone, and, later, Alvin Karpis, who would eventually serve more time on "The Rock" than any other inmate. Four years after his confinement, Doc had apparently had enough. When his attempt at escape failed and Doc was confronted by guards, he ignored their orders and just kept walking toward the waters of San Francisco Bay. Guards gunned him down. His last words reportedly were, "I'm all shot to hell."

Following Doc's arrest, agents searching his Chicago apartment discovered a map with locations circled in Florida. Regarded by agents as clues to the whereabouts of his compatriots, the find would lead the FBI directly to Doc's brother, Fred, and their mother, the notorious Ma Barker. After four long years of searching for the murderers, it would take little more than a week to locate them. The Barkers were living a life of luxury in a small rented cottage on Lake Weir near Ocala, Florida. Before dawn on January 16, 1935, federal agents had the hideout surrounded and ordered the Barkers to surrender without any further violence. Fred responded with a blast from a machine gun.

The firefight went on for hours, with hundreds of rounds fired by FBI agents and the criminals. When the smoke finally cleared, agents stormed the house, only to find both Barkers dead from gunshots. The FBI claimed that Ma Barker was found with a submachine gun in her hands, though others have discounted that contention, saying it was fabricated to justify the FBI's killing of an old woman.

Karpis had visited the Barkers at Lake Weir just weeks before their deaths, then vacationed in Havana, Cuba, before traveling to Cleveland, Miami, Atlantic City, and, lastly, New

Orleans. There, on May 2, 1936, FBI agents surrounded his apartment with machine guns, shotguns, revolvers, tear-gas guns, and bombs, and waited for him to come outside. Eventually, he did, and G-men immediately took him into custody without violence. However, supposedly used to killing public enemies and not capturing them, none of the FBI agents had brought a pair of handcuffs; instead, they used an agent's necktie to secure the suspect's hands.

Newspapers around the country celebrated the arrest with headline fonts normally reserved for the end of world wars, shouting G-MEN ARREST ALVIN KARPIS.

> Alvin Karpis, No. 1 public enemy of the nation, wanted for wholesale kidnapping, murder and robbery and with a price of $7,000 on his head, was captured tonight without bloodshed. He was not armed. The desperado was taken by a squad of G-men who lined up in firing squad formation before his apartment near the business section of New Orleans. Fred Hunter, wanted for a $85,000 mail robbery in Garrettville, Ohio, and a pretty twenty-two-year-old young woman, unidentified, were captured with him.
>
> The G-men, headed by J. Edgar Hoover, chief of the bureau of investigation of the department of justice, were out to avenge the murder of four fellow officers of which Karpis was suspected, and they took no chances.
>
> Three hours after the capture, the plane carrying 10 G-men, heavily armed, and the shackled outlaw, took off from Shushan airport for St. Paul. Hunter and the woman were left behind.
>
> Although Karpis was suspected of numerous crimes, the government wanted him especially for the kidnapping of William A. Hamm Jr., wealthy St. Paul brewer. His dramatic transfer to St. Paul was on personal orders of Hoover, chief of the G-men, who came here from New York personally to direct the capture.

Returned to the Twin Cities for trial and found guilty of kidnapping Hamm, Karpis was sentenced to life in prison at Alcatraz in 1936. He would serve thirty-three years before being paroled in 1969. Karpis lived to write his autobiography and a memoir dedicated to his time on "The Rock." Neither Karpis nor any of the Barkers were ever tried for the robberies of three Nebraska banks or the shooting of six people in the Fairbury affair.

Hatchet Man
Roland Dean Sundahl

If an outlaw is, as the dictionary defines, "a lawless person or a fugitive from the law," regardless of how long or successfully they evaded escape, then Roland Dean Sundahl was one of Nebraska's most despicable examples.

At first glance, his lone victim was a vivacious sixteen-year-old carhop who worked at a family-owned drive-in restaurant. But in the wake of his crime, Roland Sundahl left a wave of misery that wounded his two young children, his wife, and his parents, to say nothing of the family of his prey.

In 1950, twenty-year-old Sundahl seemed to have the weight of the world on his shoulders. Despite his youth, he already had a wife and two small children, and his meager wage as a laborer didn't afford him any luxuries. In fact, his young family of four was lucky to have a small, ramshackle cottage behind the home of his parents' house in Norfolk, Nebraska.

The rest of the world was still waking up in 1950, following the end of World War II. In the U.S., a booming postwar economy had returning GIs finishing college, the Dow at 235 points, cars streaming off the sales lots at 1,700 bucks a pop, with Nat King Cole crooning "Mona Lisa" on their dash-mounted radios, and *The Ed Sullivan Show* to warm Sunday-night living rooms. For many, it was, and still remains today, an idyllic existence.

At the time, Roland Sundahl lived for the weekends, when he could hop in his car, forget his needy wife and crying kids, fill the tank at 27 cents a gallon, and cruise around central Nebraska. On a sweet summer Saturday night in late August 1950, Sundahl jumped in his car in Norfolk and headed south, taking just twenty-five minutes to reach the small town of Columbus, founded a century earlier on the Mormon Pioneer Trail.

His friends were waiting, and Sundahl soon hooked up with his buddy, Cliff Burgess (fictitious name). They would cruise around town and, despite his marital status, scope out girls. One of their favorite haunts was the Y-Knot Cafe, which, in addition to offering outstanding 20-cent hamburgers, barbecued ribs, and homemade pies, had some of the cutest young women in east-central Nebraska working as carhops.

The two stopped at the drive-in cafe for burgers and sodas, and Burgess took advantage of the time to sweet-talk pretty sixteen-year-old Bonnie Lou Merrill. Before long, Bonnie had agreed to go out after work with Burgess. After all, the Labor Day weekend was fast approaching; her summer away from her Silver Creek home was coming to an end, and, in a week, she would have to head back to classes for her senior year at the high school.

When Bonnie's Saturday-night shift ended at 1:30 a.m. Sunday morning, Burgess and Sundahl were waiting for her in Sundahl's car. The cozy threesome headed out of town for some late-night fun, stopped at a roadside cafe, and drank soft drinks. When someone plugged a quarter in the jukebox, Burgess and Sundahl took turns dancing with the comely Bonnie Lou. About an hour into the adventure, Bonnie told the boys she was tired after her long shift and wanted to return to her rooming house.

Shortly after 2:30 a.m., Sundahl dropped Burgess at his car, just a couple blocks from Bonnie's apartment on the same street. Bonnie had said that she liked to be dropped off a block from her place, lest the other tenants get to talking. Burgess watched Sundahl's car proceed down the street until the brake lights illuminated, about where he suspected Bonnie wanted to be dropped off. Burgess then went home to bed.

But Roland and Bonnie didn't.

Whether Bonnie was forced to accompany Roland on a nocturnal cruise, sans Burgess, or whether she found something in the twenty-year-old laborer attractive and rode with him voluntarily, is anyone's guess. Regardless, Roland and Bonnie headed out of town to an isolated private reservoir 6 miles northwest of Columbus, called Lake Babcock. There, on the quiet lakeshore, things went south.

Even though he already had two toddlers at home, Sundahl apparently wanted to make at least one more. However, Bonnie Lou wasn't interested in being intimate, and she strenuously objected to her companion's explicit overtures. When she continued to object to Sundahl's advances and demanded to be taken home, Sundahl turned violent.

Meanwhile, some 20 miles away in her Silver Creek home, Mrs. Clifford J. Merrill, Bonnie Lou's mother, was worried. She hadn't received a telephone call from her daughter that day, which wasn't like her. Mrs. Merrill had only reluctantly allowed her daughter to go earn some summer spending money by working and living in the bigger town of Columbus.

When Sunday, Monday, and Tuesday passed with still no call from Bonnie, Mrs. Merrill became frantic. Finally, she drove herself over to Columbus to see why her daughter had been so neglectful. She soon learned that no one had even seen her teenage offspring since early Sunday morning. Now Friday morning, September 1, 1950, Mrs. Merrill immediately went to the police to report her daughter missing.

Officers quickly drove to Bonnie's boardinghouse and gained access to her room. They found everything in exceptional order, with dresses hanging tidily in the closet and Bonnie's summer savings of $80 stashed in her pocketbook.

According to *San Antonio Light* reporter Edward D. Radin, who later wrote about the case, Columbus police chief Edward Nickolite was grim when his officers reported what they had found at the young woman's apartment.

"This means that Bonnie's been murdered," he said flatly. "If she was off on some romantic escapade or decided to run away to a big city, she would have taken her things with her. She never returned to her room, so her disappearance was not voluntary. Considering her character, she must be dead; otherwise she would have gotten in touch with her mother."

With due haste, Columbus police retraced Bonnie's last known activities, and quickly learned that she had worked the late shift at the drive-in on Saturday night. A fellow waitress confided to police that Bonnie Lou had said she had set up a date after work with Cliff Burgess, a local boy.

Called in for questioning, Burgess acknowledged that he had met Bonnie after work, and that the two of them, plus a Norfolk man known as Roland Sundahl, had gone out for soft drinks and some dancing. Burgess also told investigators that Bonnie probably had gone out with him because another boy who she didn't really like, named Herman Fried (fictitious name), had been pestering her for a date that same night.

Grilled by police, Burgess said he and Sundahl had arrived at the drive-in about 1:30 a.m. in Sundahl's vehicle. He then recounted their activities, saying that Sundahl had first dropped him off, and then Bonnie, back at their places. When asked if he had seen anybody else on the street that night, Burgess said he might have spotted Fried.

Questioned separately, Sundahl essentially told the same story, except he said he hadn't seen Fried. He also turned over to police a small bottle of liquid makeup that he said belonged to Bonnie. Sundahl explained that he had asked the young girl to dance to the music of the jukebox while she was making up her face. When she stood up to dance, Sundahl said she had placed the small bottle in his pocket. He said he had forgotten to return it to her when he had dropped her off near her rooming house.

Sundahl said that after leaving Bonnie, he had returned to the drive-in. A witness verified his story. Fried, in turn, denied ever seeing Bonnie that night, and said he was with relatives. With no dead body, or any evidence to suggest that a crime had been committed, all three suspects were released.

The next day, Nickolite's dire prediction of murder came true when Bonnie's nude, nearly decapitated body was discovered hidden in some weeds at Lake Babcock. The victim clearly had struggled and been beaten about the head and neck. Skin scrapings were found under her fingernails, indicating that she had fought her attacker. Robbery was ruled out as a motive when Bonnie's small clutch purse was found with the body, still holding her tip money, lipstick, and a key to her room.

When newspapers announced the gruesome discovery of Bonnie Lou Merrill—struck down in the prime of her life, with so much still before her—it sent a chill through the spines of every Nebraska resident.

Sundahl, Burgess, and Fried were questioned again by the police, and none of them changed his story. Neither did any of them have visible scratch marks, the telltale sign that could lead investigators to the culprit.

Reporter Radin later wrote, "The chief reviewed the facts with his men and noted that a case could be built against any of the three. Fried had kept after Bonnie even though she showed no desire to date him. Sundahl was the last known person to see her alive. And Burgess, who had arranged the initial date with Bonnie, could have coordinated a later rendezvous after they had parted company with Sundahl."

But the chief would show why he was the head honcho of the local police department. Radin wrote:

> "Sundahl is the killer," Chief Nickolite said, holding up the bottle of liquid makeup. "All of us daily see women making up their faces. The last thing they apply is lipstick, *after* makeup powder. Yet, Bonnie's lipstick was in her purse. If she had time to return that, she would have replaced the makeup. I wondered why Sundahl had bothered to turn this over to us. I think he was afraid of being searched and having it found on him. He tried to throw us off by claiming it came from Bonnie."
>
> "Why?" one of his officers asked. "What's the purpose?"
>
> Chief Nickolite rasped his fingernails across the top of one hand, raising red welts. He quickly applied the liquid makeup and the blemish disappeared. "It was used as a cover-up for murder."

Law officers hastily brought Sundahl into the Columbus police department, forced him to strip to the waist, and washed him thoroughly. To their amazement, and the chief's credit, the officers watched as the long scratch marks came into view on Sundahl's forearms. In minutes, Sundahl broke down and confessed to the sordid crime, sending off a second wave of hysteria and massive press coverage.

On Sunday, September 3, Americans woke up to newspaper headlines that shouted NEBRASKA MAN ADMITS KILLING SCHOOLGIRL. In its coverage, the United Press reported:

> A young father confessed Saturday that he killed a 16-year-old high school girl who resisted his love-making, and led police to her body in weed-covered grave beside a lake.
>
> Roland Sundahl, 20, Norfolk, Neb., a father of two children, led authorities to the shore of Lake Babcock, where they found the body of pretty Bonnie Merrill, of Silver Creek, Neb. Police Chief Edward Nickolite said Sundahl confessed that he choked the girl until she went limp when she repulsed his advances in his parked car last Sunday about 4 a.m. Then he said he dragged her from the car and beat her with a hatchet, Nickolite said.

The same day, the Associated Press added, "Afterward, Sundahl went to a nearby filling station, drank a cup of coffee and slept in his car."

Outrage over the murder of such a young, innocent girl was not contained, and everyone clamored for justice. Less than two months after Bonnie Lou Merrill's body was discovered, Roland Dean Sundahl found himself on trial in Platte County District Court, charged with two counts of first-degree murder. One charged murder with a hatchet while the other charged murder with a hatchet during an attempted criminal assault.

The four-day trial included the prosecution's submittal of a confession signed by Sundahl. For his defense, attorneys argued that he was insane, while his family members testified that, in the year before the crime, Sundahl's health had changed and that he had become moody, depressed, and suffered from headaches.

A psychiatrist conducted an evaluation of the twenty-year-old accused murderer, and reported that Sundahl had a tendency to withdraw from people into "a dream world of fantasy." But a doctor testifying for the prosecution rebuffed that assertion, saying Sundahl had no history of mental illness and that he knew right from wrong.

In the surprise of the trial, Sundahl took the stand in his own defense, testifying in a quiet and calm manner that the death of Bonnie Lou Merrill, "to me is like a dream. I can't believe it was possible. Something snapped when I put my arm around her and squeezed," he said.

The excruciating testimony detailing the night of the murder, and Sundahl's horrific and brutal assault on the young girl, was too much for family members of both victim and defendant. Sundahl's mother collapsed in the courtroom on several occasions, and Sundahl's wife became hysterical and made frequent outbursts that unsettled the court.

When the testimony ended, the jury of twelve men deliberated for nine hours before returning a unanimous verdict of guilty of murder in the first degree, and recommended that the punishment should be the death penalty.

A month later, on January 6, 1951, Roland Dean Sundahl openly wept as he stood before District Court Judge R. D. Flory, who rejected all defense arguments, pronounced the death penalty, and set the execution date for April 2.

Noting that an appeal to the Nebraska State Supreme Court would likely force a postponement, the United Press reported that, "The 20-year-old father of two children today faced death in the electric chair for the hatchet slaying of a teen-aged waitress who resisted his advances. His confession said that he buried the body in a shallow grave, then went home to his wife and children in Norfolk, Neb."

The appeals process did, indeed, delay Sundahl's planned execution. But on July 6, 1951, the state Supreme Court upheld the sentence, stating there was "no justifiable reason for changing the judgment of the jury." Another appeal to the state Pardon Board, citing his youth and arguing for a commutation of the sentence to life imprisonment, was granted a hearing in mid-April 1952, but the board ruled against the commutation. With that, Sundahl's fate was sealed.

On April 30, 1952, just twenty months after the killing, Roland Sundahl would pay the ultimate price for his hideous crime. In newspaper stories carried across the U.S., the United Press reported:

> Bible-reading Roland D. Sundahl walked calmly to his death in the electric chair Wednesday for the hatchet murder of a teen-age car-hop.
>
> Sundahl, the 21-year-old father of two, was pronounced dead at 12:07 a.m. (CST) after 2,250 volts of electricity surged through his body.
>
> His death ended pleas for commutation of his sentence which had set back his execution date four times since he was convicted of murdering Bonnie Lou Merrill, of Silver Creek, Neb., in 1950.
>
> Since then the Norfolk, Neb., youth had spent his days reading the Bible, comic books and westerns, and listening to the radio.

He had confessed [to] murdering Miss Merrill, a 16-year-old high school girl who worked part-time as a drive-in car-hop, near Columbus, Neb. after the girl had resisted his advances during an automobile ride.

His electrocution took place in a garishly lighted basement room under the offices of Warden Herbert Hann of the state penitentiary. Sundahl replied "no" in an almost inaudible murmur when Hann asked him if he had any last words. Then the warden gave the signal and an unidentified executioner threw the switch.

Charles Starkweather and the End of Innocence

The mystique of Charles Starkweather still hangs over Nebraska like a storm cloud a half-century after his early demise. Lincoln residents who were children then can still recall the outlaw's exploits, the day the governor called out the National Guard, and the time their parents pulled them out of school because they feared for their lives.

Starkweather remains historically important not only because he thought of himself as a modern-day outlaw, but because in a matter of three days, he left in his wake ten bodies, becoming the first of the contemporary serial killers who murdered for pure sport. The pure randomness of the killer's actions sent the populace into a frenzy.

Charles Starkweather's deadly antics would spawn hundreds of newspaper articles, books, and eventually even a network television miniseries. During the course of a week in Nebraska's capital city, Charles Starkweather had the attention of nearly every one of its 128,000 residents. Businesses closed, students were kept home from school, and locals purchased virtually every rifle, shotgun, pistol, and box of ammunition in the state of Nebraska.

That a nineteen-year-old ninth-grade dropout could create such fury and fear was nothing short of astounding. Starkweather would prove that being dumb and disenfranchised could have deadly implications.

As the fall of 1957 turned to another frozen winter on the Nebraska prairie, teenager Charles Starkweather was self-medicating with a combination of Wild Turkey and malt beverages, the remains of which were scattered throughout his ramshackle tenement house in a poor neighborhood of Lincoln, Nebraska. He was cold, hungry, broke, and suffering from another in an endless series of headaches that had plagued him for years.

Fumbling with a box of shotgun shells, he picked up a Remington 12-gauge pump-action shotgun he had "borrowed" from a friend's garage the day before and loaded it with three shells, ejecting them one by one on the dirty floor of his small apartment. As he did so, he thought about his empty wallet, his dead-end job as a garbage hauler paying just $42 a week, and the lack of respect virtually everyone in his life showed him. Well, he'd show them.

Meanwhile, a few blocks away, Robert Colvert was working the overnight shift at the Crest Service Station, among the newest and brightest on Lincoln's Cornhusker Highway. Just discharged from the Navy, the twenty-one-year-old had been happy to land a job where he could work on cars and support his family. "Little Bob," as his friends called him, had a nineteen-year-old wife at home, and they were expecting their first child. Life was good.

When Charles Starkweather pulled his blue Ford into the Crest Service Station shortly after 3:00 a.m. on December 1, 1957, Colvert was in the service bay, rebuilding a carburetor. When he heard Starkweather enter the store and yell for some assistance, he wiped his greasy hands on a rag, went to the counter, and sold the young man a pack of Camels for a quarter. Then Starkweather turned, walked out the door of the gas station, jumped in his car, and drove away. Colvert went back to his late-night work. A few minutes later, Starkweather returned, bought a pack of gum, and headed back to his car.

Confident that he had thoroughly "cased" the joint, the red-headed Starkweather affected his disguise, donning a hunting cap pulled low to his eyes, leather gloves, and a red bandana tied tightly around his face. Then he loaded his shotgun, climbed out of the car, and strolled back into the service station. Working on the car out back, Colvert didn't hear Starkweather return. When he felt the barrel of a shotgun touch the back of his head, he turned to see a masked man pointing a 12-gauge at his face. Leading Colvert into the office, Starkweather ordered him to dim the bright floodlights out front and clean out the cash register. Colvert did as ordered, stuffing a minuscule $96 in currency and $12 in coin into a bank bag Starkweather had supplied for the occasion.

The state's newest criminal then pointed the shotgun at Colvert and ordered him to get in his car and drive. Colvert did as instructed, undoubtedly wondering where this night with a well-armed bandit would lead. Driving northeast of Lincoln on a Lancaster County road, Starkweather told Colvert to stop the car near some railroad tracks and get out. The gunman followed his hostage through the driver's side door, with malicious intent. Colvert realized that he was in mortal danger and lunged for the shotgun. In the ensuing struggle, Starkweather was able to wrest the gun away from Colvert, aim, and fire. The force of the blast sent the young victim flying, and he landed facedown in the frozen road.

Despite the severe wound inflicted by the shotgun discharge, Colvert struggled to regain his feet. Starkweather wasn't letting him go anywhere. The boy ejected the spent shell and reloaded, then placed the barrel against the back of Colvert's head and squeezed the trigger again. On that lonely county road, Colvert's wife became a widow and his yet-unborn son became fatherless.

With adrenaline surging through his bloodstream, Starkweather tossed his shotgun in the car, jumped behind the wheel, and tore away. A mile down the road, he realized he had left the shell casing from his first shot on the ground. Returning to the scene, he drove up to the bleeding body of his victim, hopped out, and retrieved the shell. Then, without taking another look at the damage he had inflicted, he drove off into the night.

By 5:00 a.m., Lincoln police officers were at the Crest Service Station, wondering why no one was working. A short time later, Colvert's body was discovered lying in the road just outside city limits.

Four hours later, Starkweather was with his fourteen-year-old girlfriend, Caril Ann Fugate, and during their conversation, he let it slip that he was flush with coin and had robbed the service station the previous night. Young and rebellious, Fugate admired her boyfriend's ambition and his willingness to do what it took to get the job done. The couple took a leisurely drive in Starkweather's car, dumped the shotgun in a remote creek, and drove back downtown. Stopping at a used clothing store, Starkweather picked out some new-to-him clothing, including jeans and a warm shirt. He paid for his $9.55 purchase with coins grabbed from the bank bag.

While the Lincoln Police Department was searching for clues to help solve Colvert's murder, Charlie was busy too.

A fan of gangster movies then in vogue, he changed his car tires, painted his Ford black, and removed the grille and painted that portion red, hoping it would make the vehicle used in the commission of his crime harder to trace. Worried that police would discover his discarded gun, he returned to the creek and waded through the frigid water until he had retrieved the shotgun. Returning to his tenement house, he thoroughly cleaned the weapon and returned it to the garage of his friend's house, undetected.

Nine days after the murder, Charlie and Caril even stopped at the Crest Service Station and purchased a small stuffed poodle for her. Feeling as if they had more money than ever before, they splurged, seeing movies, buying junk food and rock 'n' roll 45s, and hanging out in his apartment. The two young lovers became closer than ever, bonded in their conspiracy of robbery and murder in the heartland.

Five weeks later, Starkweather was broke, having been fired from his trash-hauling job. He'd been evicted from his apartment for failure to pay his rent, forced to sleep in his car even though temperatures dipped below freezing at night. Sick, hungry, and without a good night's sleep since the padlock had been placed on his tenement door, Starkweather was at the end of his rope. So, he drove over to his brother's house and borrowed his .22 caliber rifle, telling his brother he was going hunting.

He drove over to Caril's house and sat in his car while he finished his cigarette. He stuck two boxes of .22 shells into his jacket pocket and grabbed the rifle as he exited the Ford, making his way to the door. He was greeted with disgust by Caril Ann's mother, Mrs. Velda Bartlett. As she glared at him,

Charlie set the rifle down in the corner of the kitchen. When Mrs. Bartlett told Starkweather she never wanted Caril to see him again, the young man asked why. Mrs. Bartlett slapped Charlie twice across the face and then told him he had gotten the fourteen-year-old pregnant. Stunned by the news and Mrs. Bartlett's attack, Charlie returned to his car and drove around the block to cool down.

Remembering his rifle, Charlie drove back to Caril's house, forced his way past Velda at the back door, and strode into the kitchen to get his gun. There stood Marion Bartlett, Caril's powerfully built stepfather. The older man ordered Charlie to get out of his house and provided a good kick in the butt to help him on his way.

Fuming, Charlie left the house without his gun, and, in his feeble way, began executing a plan for revenge. He stopped at a pay phone and called Marion's employer, the Watson Brothers Transportation Co., and informed them that Marion Bartlett was sick and wouldn't be coming to work for a few days.

Charlie then got back into his car, dropped it a block from the Bartlett house, and walked to the scene of his next grisly crime. Forcing his way through the back door, he found Caril arguing with her mother in the kitchen. Caril's two-year-old sister, Betty Jean, was at her mother's side. When Caril saw her boyfriend, she ran into the bathroom and slammed the door. Charlie continued verbally sparring with Velda Bartlett until the exasperated woman again slapped Charlie twice across the face.

At his limit, Charlie made a fist and punched Caril's mother, knocking her to the floor. Just then, Marion entered to see his wife being pummeled. He immediately went to her aid, grabbing Charlie by the neck and flipping him over his back. Marion then picked up the young man and carted him toward the front door. But Charlie fought back, freed himself of the step-father's grip, and fled to Caril's bedroom. There he found the .22 rifle, grabbed a bullet from his pocket, loaded the gun, and turned his head toward the door, just as Marion entered with a claw hammer raised over his head. Starkweather didn't hesitate. He raised the gun, pulled the trigger, and watched as Marion slumped to the floor with blood streaming from his head.

Hearing the shot, Velda grabbed a large butcher knife and ran to her husband's side. When Charlie told her not to take another step, Velda ignored him, and Charlie fired another round from the gun. The round struck Caril's mother in the face and she stumbled into the living room, blood gushing from her head. Sensing another kill, Charlie followed Velda into the living room, turned his rifle around, and struck Velda in the face repeatedly with the butt of the gun until she fell silent, a bloody heap on the floor.

Little Betty Jean, bawling at the violence all around her, was silenced in the same manner. When he heard moans coming from Caril's bedroom, Charlie returned there with Velda's knife, plunging it to the hilt into Marion's neck until he, too, fell silent.

Examining the carnage he had created, Charlie calmly walked about the house collecting sheets, blankets, and rugs. He then wrapped each of the bodies individually, tying them tight with clothesline, and dragged them out onto the back porch. With Caril's assistance, they stashed Mr. Bartlett's body in the chicken coop in the backyard. They stuffed Mrs. Bartlett's corpse as far down into the outhouse privy as it would go, and set little Betty Jean's body on the privy's toilet seat.

The couple then returned to the house, rearranged the furniture, wiped up the blood, watched a little television, and, later, walked to the local grocery store for some soft drinks and potato chips. That night, Charlie and Caril fell asleep in each other's arms, just the two of them against the world.

For the next six days, the two played house, occasionally walking to the grocery store for more snack foods, feeding the dogs and the parakeet, watching TV, playing gin rummy, and shooing away visitors by saying everyone in the house was extremely sick.

By week's end, schoolmates, neighbors, and even Marion's boss and Caril's older sister were stopping by with increasing frequency. Finally, the police arrived at about 9:25 p.m., on January 25, in response to a call of concern from Caril's brother-in-law. Knocking on the door, it opened to reveal Caril in a nightgown, looking as if she had just woken up. When questioned, Caril gave the police very convincing answers, explaining that her parents and little sister were sick with the flu, and didn't want any visitors. The police left the Bartlett home and made a standard report on their welfare check in the Belmont subdivision of Lincoln.

Meanwhile, Charlie, now heavily armed with a sawed-off shotgun, handgun, and rifle, hid out in the Bartlett bathroom.

Concerned over the police attention and recurring visits from frustrated family members, Charlie decided it was time to fly the coop. Packing up a few belongings and all of their guns, the two walked a block to Charlie's car. After changing a flat tire, the two stopped at a service station across the street from the State Highway Patrol and the State Penitentiary and had the car's transmission serviced. They stopped at a roadside cafe for burgers, and bought more bullets at a service station. Then they headed out of town, to a small farm where Charlie had often hunted, with the owner's permission.

As Charlie and Caril approached the farm of elderly August Meyer, recent snow made the dirt road virtually impassable, and soon, they were stuck up to the axles. They exited the car and began trudging through the snow toward Meyer's farmhouse. Along the way, they checked out the ruins of an old schoolhouse, its foundation and storm cellar the only remnants of the old building.

When they reached Meyer's house, they found the old bachelor finishing a sandwich in his kitchen. Harsh words were exchanged between the two men. Charlie was tense from the last several days, and mad about getting his car stuck in the farmer's lane. Meyer decided he didn't have to take any lip from a bow-legged punk who combed his hair like James Dean. When Charlie and Caril left the farmhouse, Meyer followed them outside, carrying a rifle. This spooked Charlie, who raised his sawed-off shotgun and shot his old farmer friend right in the face, killing him instantly. Then he shot the farmer's dog, too.

After stashing Meyer's body in a shed, the two went inside the house for something to eat. While Caril explored the kitchen, Charlie ransacked the house, looking for money and more firepower.

On that same afternoon of Monday, January 27, family members visiting the Bartlett house in Lincoln stumbled on the remains of Marion and Velda Bartlett and their tiny daughter, Betty Jean. Police immediately issued an alert to pick up for questioning a Charles R. Starkweather and a Caril Ann Fugate, and gave a description of Charlie's car, right down to the red grille and the license-plate number.

Charlie had spent an hour freezing on Meyer's muddy road, trying to get his car unstuck. When he finally succeeded, he again got stuck farther down the lane. With the help of a local rancher, who used a cable and his own vehicle to pull Charlie's car out of the muck, Charlie was able to get his car back on dryer ground.

When Charlie and Caril got stuck for a third time, Charlie's blood pressure skyrocketed. As they walked down a muddy road with darkness falling, a young high school couple, Robert Jensen, seventeen, and his girlfriend, Carol King, sixteen, stopped their car and asked if they could be of assistance. It was an unfortunate time to be Good Samaritans. Still well armed, Charlie and Caril took the two as hostages and made them drive to the old schoolhouse ruins. There, they shot and stabbed the young couple and stuffed their bloody bodies in the storm cellar, driving away in Jensen's car.

Returning to Lincoln, Charlie and Caril spent the night sleeping in the stolen vehicle on a neighborhood street. As dawn arrived in southeastern Nebraska, they awoke and made plans for the day. The first order of business was acquiring enough cash to make their getaway. Familiar with the posh neighborhoods of Lincoln that he had serviced as a garbageman, Charlie headed for the country club section of town and simply drove up the driveway of a two-story mansion in one of its most affluent neighborhoods.

The outlaws had picked the home of one of Lincoln's most prosperous businessmen, C. Lauer Ward, the forty-seven-year-old president of two major companies, and his wife, forty-six-year-old Clara Ward. The only other full-time resident was Lillian Fencl, the Wards' maid of more than a quarter-century. When Ms. Fencl answered the knock at the back door, she was greeted by the barrel of Charlie's .22 caliber rifle. Forcing his way into the kitchen at gunpoint, among the first things Charlie noticed was that day's edition of the *Lincoln Star* sitting on the table, with its bold front-page headline: BELMONT FAMILY SLAIN.

Minutes later, Clara Ward walked into the kitchen in her housecoat, ready for breakfast. Instead, she found Charles Starkweather with a gun pointed directly at her head. Charlie assured Mrs. Ward that he and Caril would stay until nightfall, tie them up, and leave them unharmed. While this was occurring, a full-scale search had been mounted for the two missing teens from Bennet, Nebraska, Jensen and King. During the search, police discovered Starkweather's car still stuck on August Meyer's farm road.

As morning turned to afternoon at the Ward house, Mrs. Ward asked Charlie if she and the maid could do some housework. Later, Clara Ward asked if she might go upstairs and change her shoes into something more comfortable. Distracted by a headache, the newspaper headlines naming he and Caril fugitives, and a quick note he decided to jot down for police, some time had passed before Charlie realized Mrs. Ward hadn't yet returned from upstairs. As he climbed the stairway swearing under his breath, Mrs. Ward calmly stepped from a doorway, aimed a rifle at him, and fired.

The bullet struck the wall inches from Charlie's head. After Mrs. Ward threw the rifle at him and ran for the stairs, Charlie took a long knife from his boot and heaved it at the fleeing woman. The knife struck Mrs. Ward in the middle of her back and she fell. Walking to the wounded woman, Charlie examined his perfect aim, pulled the knife from her back, picked up the moaning Mrs. Ward, and threw her in a bedroom. When her black poodle bared its teeth at him to protect its master, Charlie swung his rifle and broke the dog's neck. He then tore sheets into strips and tied Mrs. Ward securely to the bed, after which he stabbed her to death.

Meanwhile, law officers had converged on August Meyer's farm after discovering Starkweather's Ford. They soon found Meyer's body in an outbuilding. An hour and a half later, a neighbor of Meyer's searched the old schoolhouse storm cellar and found the bodies of the missing teenagers. The body count was rising, and the news prompted the governor to call out the National Guard to blanket the streets, as armed parents picked up their children early from school.

Charlie and Caril spent the afternoon ransacking the Ward house for valuables and clipping articles about their foray into crime from the front page of the *Lincoln Journal*. When Mr. Ward came home from work, Charlie met him at the door with a loaded rifle, then shot him in the back when he attempted to escape. Then he took the maid to an upstairs bedroom, tied her down, and repeatedly stabbed her until she was dead. When he was finished with his gruesome work, and covered in blood, he asked Caril to get him a clean shirt from Mr. Ward's closet.

Worried that neighbors might have heard the gunshots, Charlie and Caril packed up the Wards' 1956 Packard, backed out of the driveway, and by 8:00 p.m., they were on their way to Washington State, taking the back roads to avoid police. By 4:00 a.m., Charlie was dozing at the wheel and momentarily fell asleep, sending the big sedan into the ditch. When he finally regained control and steered back onto the blacktop, he knew he'd have to stop and sleep for a while.

The next morning, with a Bennet, Nebraska, dateline, the *Omaha World-Herald* reported that "Terror stalked the countryside Tuesday night. Farm houses became armed camps and grim-lipped men and women here, 16 miles southeast of Lincoln, burned lights far past the usual bedtime."

Before sunup on January 29, 1958, the Packard rambled past Chadron westward until it crossed the Nebraska-Wyoming state line, where Charlie slowed down. Listening to the radio, Charlie and Caril learned that the bodies of the Wards and their maid had been discovered. The newscaster also announced that the fugitives might be driving a 1956 Packard.

A few miles later, Charlie noticed a late-model Buick parked just off the highway and realized it might be his best chance to switch cars. He stopped, walked up to the car, and found Merle Collison, a thirty-seven-year-old shoe salesman from Great Falls, Montana, asleep at the wheel. Collison refused to unlock his door, so Charlie retrieved one of his .22 rifles, returned to the Buick, and shot through the closed window, hitting the traveling salesman in the head and neck. When Charlie's gun jammed, he went back to the Packard, retrieved another rifle, and shot Collison seven more times.

Just then, Joe Sprinkle happened on the scene. A young geologist from Casper, Wyoming, Sprinkle spotted two late-model cars on the side of the road and thought he ought to stop and see if they needed help. When he inquired, Charlie greeted him in return with the business end of his rifle. Noticing the dead body slumped in the passenger side of the front seat, Sprinkle immediately realized his life was in danger and grabbed for the barrel of the gun. A lengthy life-and-death struggle ensued, with the six-foot Sprinkle locking his hands on the gun and refusing to let go. With Sprinkle's car blocking one lane of the highway, two vehicles on the shoulder, and two men fighting in the middle of the road for control of a rifle, it was difficult for Natrona County, Wyoming, deputy sheriff Bill Romer to miss the altercation when he drove up.

Before the deputy could even draw his service revolver, Caril jumped from the Buick and hysterically ran to his patrol car, screaming, "He's going to kill me! He's going to kill me! He already killed one man!" When asked who was going to kill her, the girl sobbed, "Charles Starkweather is going to kill me!" The deputy dragged the girl to his car and placed her inside.

Finally seeing the deputy's cruiser stopped nearby, Charlie ended his fight with Sprinkle and ran for the Packard. With tires squealing, Charles Starkweather, the most wanted man in the Midwest, tried to make his daring escape by heading west. But it's hard to outrun a radio. Deputy Romer called the dispatch center for the Wyoming Highway Patrol, alerted them to the situation, and called for all troopers to converge on Douglas to capture Starkweather. Although he followed the fleeing murder suspect for several miles, Romer eventually broke off pursuit and returned to the scene of Collison's murder.

Based on the description of the vehicle provided by Deputy Romer, Douglas police spotted the Packard moving at a high rate of speed as it raced through town. Pursuing it west at speeds approaching 120 mph, Douglas police chief Robert Ainslie drove as Sheriff Early Heflin fired his .30-30 rifle out the window. Heflin succeeded in shattering the Packard's rear

Mass murderer Charles Starkweather smokes a cigarette after being captured by Wyoming lawmen in January 1958. *Photo courtesy of the Nebraska State Historical Society*

window, and a short time later, the law enforcement officers drove over a rise to find the Packard stopped in the middle of the highway. Charlie stepped out of the vehicle and stood facing the police car. When it looked as if he might get back in the car, Chief Ainslie fired a couple of rounds from his revolver to convince Starkweather that doing anything other than lying on the ground might not be prudent.

Charles Starkweather's eight-day murder spree had finally ended.

The morning after Starkweather's capture, the *Omaha World-Herald*'s banner headline screamed PUNK'S BLOOD-STAINED STRING ENDS AT 10 DEAD WITH WYOMING CAPTURE. And, as one local resident would later write, "Now Lincoln's parents had a local poster of the kind of teenager they didn't want their daughters to date."

The verdict in Starkweather's case was all but a foregone conclusion when he went to trial just three months after his arrest. He was convicted of killing the two high school students and was sentenced to death. Caril was charged and convicted of the same crimes, though her attorneys argued that she was an unwilling captive who played no part in the murders. Jurors weren't convinced and found her guilty. On November 21, 1958, she became the youngest woman in the U.S. to ever be sentenced to life in prison. She would be paroled in 1976, move to Michigan, and forever after, maintain her innocence.

After a series of appeals that lasted just over a year, Charles Starkweather walked to the Nebraska death chamber only a year and a half after his conviction. In newspaper accounts carried across the U.S., the Associated Press reported on June 25, 1959:

> Mass murderer Charles Starkweather, calm and almost cocky to the end, paid with his life early Thursday for a killing rampage that shocked the nation 18 months ago.
>
> Death in the electric chair at 12:05 a.m. closed out the infamous career of the 20-year-old ex-garbage hauler whose confessions involved him in 11 knife and gun killings.
>
> The end came at the Nebraska State Penitentiary after a day of frantic efforts by the killer's parents and Washington attorneys to gain a new reprieve. Starkweather had no last words.
>
> "Is there anything you would like to say?" Deputy Warden John Greenholtz asked. Strapped in the massive wooden electric chair, Starkweather shook his head negatively.
>
> At 12:01 a.m. the young killer, his head shaven and one trouser leg rolled up to permit electrical contact,

walked into the basement execution chamber. Glancing at the 35 assembled witnesses, Starkweather managed a sort of half-smile.

A curtain was drawn as the killer was strapped into the chair. The executioner, operating behind a wall out of sight of the witnesses, sent five separate charges of 2,200 volts of electricity through the heavyset redhead's body.

At each charge, Starkweather strained against his bonds. Dr. B. A. Finkel, the prison physician who was to have pronounced Starkweather dead, himself suffered a heart attack and died shortly before the execution. A substitute doctor hurriedly took his place.

Deputy Warden Greenholtz said Starkweather's last words when prison officials came to fetch him for his date with death, were, "What's your hurry?"

As Starkweather walked calmly to his death for the worst murder rampage in Nebraska history, a band of fifty teenagers gathered outside the penitentiary walls, with rock 'n' roll rhythms blaring from their car radios. Prison officials quickly dispersed the crowd.

It would be thirty-five years before Nebraska used its electric chair again.

Bibliography

Blackbird's Gruesome Game

Sheldon, Addison Erwin. *History and Stories of Nebraska.* Chicago, IL: The University Publishing Co., 1914.

Sam Bass—Scourge of the Plains

"Amazing Story of Sam Bass and Hidden Treasure West of Prairie Dell Told in Detail," *Temple News,* August 22, 1933.

Digesualdo, Jane H. and Karen R. Thompson. *Historical Round Rock.* Austin, TX: Eakin Publications, Inc., 1985.

Fifer, Barbara. *Bad Boys of the Black Hills.* Helena, MT: Farcountry Press, 2008.

O'Neal, Bill. "The Sam Bass Gang in Round Rock," *True West, 61* (February 1989).

"Sam Bass," FrontierTimes.com.

Sam Bass 100 Years Later. Round Rock, TX: Sam Bass Centennial Commission, 1978.

Smith, Helena Huntington. "Sam Bass and the Myth Machine," *The American West, 31* (January 1970).

Webb, Walter Prescott. *The Texas Rangers: A Century of Frontier Defense.* Austin, TX: University of Texas Press, 1965.

Webb, Walter Prescott, and Nicholas Eggenhofer. *The Story of the Texas Rangers.* Austin, TX: The Encino Press, 1971.

Bibliography

Wild Bill and the McCanles Brothers

Nichols, Col. George Ward. "Wild Bill," *Harper's New Monthly Magazine*, New York City (February 1867).

Patterson, Richard. *Historical Atlas of the Outlaw West.* Boulder, CO: Johnson Publishing Company, 1985.

Rosa, Joseph G. *They Called Him Wild Bill.* Norman, OK: University of Oklahoma Press, 1964, 1974.

————. *Wild Bill Hickok: The Man & His Myth.* Lawrence: University Press of Kansas, 1996.

Turner, Thadd M. *Wild Bill Hickok: Deadwood City—End of the Trail.* Boca Raton, FL: Old West Alive! Publishing, 2001.

The Doc Middleton Gang

Fifer, Barbara. *Bad Boys of the Black Hills.* Helena, MT: Farcountry Press, 2008.

Grimm, Steve. *James M. Riley Biography*, WildWestHistory .org, October 2009.

Hutton, Harold. *Doc Middleton: Life and Legends of the Notorious Plains Outlaw.* Chicago, IL: Swallow Press, 1974.

Weiser, Kathy. *Doc Middleton: King of the Horse Thieves.* LegendsofAmerica.com, December 2008.

The Demise of Kid Wade

Burdick, Fern. *Days of Yore: Early History of Brown County* (1937).

Bibliography

Faulkner, Virginia. *Roundup*. Lincoln: Bison Books, University of Nebraska Press, 1957.

Hutton, Harold. *Doc Middleton: Life and Legends of the Notorious Plains Outlaw*. Chicago, IL: Swallow Press, 1974.

———. *Vigilante Days: Frontier Justice along the Niobrara*. Chicago, IL: Swallow Press, 1978.

Flatnose Currie and the Wild Bunch

Ernst, Donna B. *The Sundance Kid: The Life of Harry Alonzo Longabaugh*. Norman, OK: University of Oklahoma Press, 2009.

Nash, Jay Robert. *Encyclopedia of Western Lawmen & Outlaws*. New York: Marlowe & Co., 1992.

"Wild Bunch," *Britannica Student Encyclopedia*.

Charles Wesley Cox and Goldie Williams

Associated Press. "Alleged Slayer of Child Taken after 25 Years," *The Independent* (Helena, Montana), June 29, 1937.

———. "Held as Slayer of Little Girl," *Lincoln Daily Journal* (Lincoln, Nebraska), February 10, 1912.

———. "No Remorse Displayed by Confessed Killer," *Las Vegas Daily Optic* (Las Vegas, New Mexico), June 28, 1937.

Colorado State Archives. Department of Corrections database, 2010.

Bibliography

"Governor Offers a Reward," *Weekly News-Journal* (Norfolk, Nebraska), February 9, 1912.

"Grand Island Child's Ravished Body Found," *Weekly News-Journal* (Norfolk, Nebraska), February 9, 1912.

"Hallam, Nebraska Tornado," *Lincoln Daily News* (Lincoln, Nebraska), June 15, 1912.

"Hold Two Murder Suspects," *The News-Palladium* (Benton Harbor, Michigan), February 12, 1912.

"Police Unable to Find Trace of Man Who Killed Goldie Williams at Grand Island (Neb.)," *The Daily Free Press* (Carbondale, Illinois), February 12, 1912.

"Slayer of Girl Not Found," *Sheboygan Journal* (Sheboygan, Wisconsin), February 10, 1912.

"Strange Coincidence Causes Damage Action," *The Evening Gazette* (Cedar Rapids, Iowa), March 13, 1912.

"Sues Telegraph Company for Delivery Mistake," *Correctionville News* (Correctionville, Iowa), October 23, 1913.

Frank "The Omaha Sniper" Carter

Associated Press. "Maniac Gunman Murders Doctor," *Oakland Tribune* (Oakland, California), February 18, 1926.

———. "Phantom Sniper Now in Custody," *Indiana Evening Gazette* (Indiana, Pennsylvania), February 23, 1926.

———. "Police Up in the Air, Residents Terror-stricken, at Mercy of Killer," *Waterloo Evening Courier* (Waterloo, Iowa), February 19, 1926.

Bibliography

"Frank 'The Omaha Sniper' Carter," *Omaha World-Herald Magazine* (Omaha, Nebraska), April 15, 1951.

"Make Last Hour Move for Carter: Attorney to Appeal to Supreme Court," *Nebraska State Journal* (Lincoln, Nebraska), June 23, 1927.

"Reports Carter 'Moral Imbecile': Brain Specialist Reveals His Findings," *Nebraska State Journal* (Lincoln, Nebraska), June 25, 1927.

" 'Sniper' Carter Near Death Door," *Nebraska State Journal* (Lincoln, Nebraska), June 22, 1927.

United Press. "Sniper Formerly Convict at Iowa Prison, Revealed," *Cedar Rapids Republican* (Cedar Rapids, Iowa), February 25, 1926.

Grandma Terror—Annie Cook

Lears, Jackson. *Rebirth of a Nation: The Making of Modern America, 1877–1920*. New York: HarperCollins Publishers, 2009.

Sehnert, Walt. "Annie Cook and Her Evil Obsession," *McCook Daily Gazette* (McCook, Nebraska), April 27, 2009.

Yost, Nellie Snyder. *Evil Obsession: The Annie Cook Story*. Lincoln, NE: Dageforde Publishing, Inc., 1991.

The Ma Barker Gang

Associated Press. "Bank Robbers Get $163,000 This Week in Nebraska Raids," *Billings Gazette* (Billings, Montana), April 9, 1933.

Bibliography

"Attempt on Life of Taran by Bomb," *The Brainerd Daily Dispatch* (Brainerd, Minnesota), December 13, 1934.

"Bandits Open Fire Felling 3," *The Brainerd Daily Dispatch* (Brainerd, Minnesota), December 16, 1932.

"Courts Catch Up With Sam Taran, Elusive Ex-Fighter," *La Crosse Tribune and Leader-Press* (La Crosse, Wisconsin), April 24, 1936.

deFord, Miriam Allen. *The Real Ma Barker*. New York: Ace Publishing Corp., 1970.

"Former Boxer Hurt in Jail Free-for-All," *The Bismarck Tribune* (Bismarck, North Dakota), December 30, 1937.

Hallberg, William. "Edward Bremer Released By Kidnappers," *Altoona Mirror* (Altoona, Pennsylvania), February 8, 1934.

"Hold Finance Head Robbery Charge," *The Brainerd Daily Dispatch* (Brainerd, Minnesota), May 8, 1933.

Hoover, J. Edgar, with Ken Jones. "The Toughest Mob We Ever Cracked," from *The FBI In Action*, Salem Press, Pasadena, CA, 1957.

Karpis, Alvin, with Bill Trent. *The Alvin Karpis Story*. New York: Berkley Medallion, 1972.

"Mill City Policeman Shot in Bank Holdup," *The Evening Tribune* (Albert Lea, Minnesota), December 16, 1932.

"Money Is Stolen By Bank Robbers," *The Daily Mail* (Hagerstown, Maryland), April 5, 1933.

"Raiders Use Machine Gun to Shoot Way Clear in Nebraska Robbery, *The Bismarck Tribune* (Bismarck, North Dakota), April 4, 1933.

United Press. "Fairbury, Neb. Bank Robbed of $27,613," *Oelwein Daily Register* (Oelwein, Iowa), April 4, 1933.

———. "Federals Surround New Orleans Apartment and Capture Public Enemy No. 1 and Companions," *Nevada State Journal* (Reno, Nevada), May 2, 1936.

Hatchet Man—Roland Dean Sundahl

Associated Press. "Court Upholds Death Sentence of Nebraskan," *The Daily Republic* (Mitchell, South Dakota), July 6, 1951.

———. "Father of Two Chokes Car-Hop," *The Daily Inter Lake* (Kalispell, Montana), September. 3, 1950.

Radin, Edward D. "Make-Up for Murder," *San Antonio Light* (San Antonio, Texas), August 31, 1958.

Schulz, Trisha. "Norfolk Man Executed before Starkweather," *Norfolk Daily News* (Norfolk, Nebraska), August 10, 2009.

United Press. "Electrocute Boy for Murdering Girl Car-Hop," *Mitchell Daily Republic* (Mitchell, South Dakota), April 30, 1952.

———. "Father of Two Faces Death in Electric Chair," *Ames Daily Tribune* (Ames, Iowa), January 6, 1951.

———. "Nebraska Man Admits Killing School Girl," *Wisconsin State Journal* (Madison, Wisconsin), September 3, 1950.

———. "Sundahl Faces Death for Hatchet Slaying," *Galveston Daily News* (Galveston, Texas), December 3, 1950.

Bibliography

Charles Starkweather and the End of Innocence

Associated Press. "Fugate: 'I am the 12th Victim,' " *The Lincoln Star* (Lincoln, Nebraska), May 1993.

———. "Killer of 11 is Calm to the End," *Waterloo Daily Courier* (Waterloo, Iowa), June 25, 1959.

———. "Nebraska Mass Slayer of 11 Is Executed," *Billings Gazette* (Billings, Montana), June 25, 1959.

O'Donnell, Jeff. *Starkweather: A Story of Mass Murder on the Great Plains.* Lincoln, NE: J&L Lee Publishers, 1993.

Piller, Dan. "Starkweather Jarred Lincoln out of '50s Tranquility," *Fort Worth Star-Telegram* (Fort Worth, Texas), May 3, 1993.

"Punk's Blood-Stained String Ends at 10 Dead With Wyoming Capture," *Omaha World-Herald* (Omaha, Nebraska), January 30, 1958.

"Starkweather Indelible in Crime History," *Lincoln Evening Journal* (Lincoln, Nebraska), December 1, 1967.

Index

Index

Index

Index

Index

Index

Index

Index

About the Author

Tom Griffith is a fourth-generation South Dakotan who studied literature and drama at the University of London before graduating with a degree in journalism from the University of Wisconsin-Eau Claire. After working as a reporter, photographer, and managing editor at newspapers in Montana, Arizona, and South Dakota, Griffith helped launch the Mount Rushmore Preservation Fund, a nationwide campaign that raised $25 million to preserve, enhance, and interpret the mountain memorial.

Griffith has written or co-authored more than fifty books, including Globe Pequot's *Insider's Guide to South Dakota's Black Hills & Badlands*, *Outlaw Tales of South Dakota*, and *Deadwood: The Best Writings on the Most Notorious Town in the West*, as well as *America's Shrine of Democracy* with a foreword by President Ronald Reagan, *A Winning Tradition* with a foreword by NBC's Tom Brokaw, and *South Dakota*, a comprehensive guide to the state. Griffith's travel features and photography have appeared in numerous magazines and newspapers from New Zealand to New York.

Griffith lives and writes in the highest reaches of South Dakota's fabled Black Hills.